John Lyly's
Mother Bombie:
A Retelling
David Bruce

This is a work of fiction. Similarities to real people, places, or events are entirely coincidental.

JOHN LYLY'S MOTHER BOMBIE: A RETELLING

First edition. December 27, 2022.

Copyright © 2022 David Bruce.

ISBN: 979-8215308073

Written by David Bruce.

Table of Contents

Copyright 2022 by Bruce D. Bruce

Do you know a language other than English? If you do, I give you permission to translate this book, copyright your translation, publish or self-publish it, and keep all the royalties for yourself. (Do give me credit, of course, for the original retelling.)

I would like to see my retellings of classic literature used in schools, so I give permission to the country of Finland (and all other countries) to give copies of any or all of my retellings to all students forever. I also give permission to the state of Texas (and all other states) to give copies of any or all of my retellings to all students forever. I also give permission to all teachers to give copies of any or all of my retellings to all students forever. Of course, libraries are welcome to use my eBooks.

Teachers need not actually teach my retellings. Teachers are welcome to give students copies of my eBooks as background material. For example, if they are teaching Homer's *Iliad* and *Odyssey*, teachers are welcome to give students copies of my *Virgil's* Aeneid: *A Retelling in Prose* and tell students, "Here's another ancient epic you may want to read in your spare time."

CAST OF CHARACTERS

FEMALE CHARACTERS

Mother Bombie, a fortune-teller, an aged cunning woman

Vicinia, a nurse, mother to Maestius and Serena

Livia, daughter to Prisius, in love with Candius

Serena, daughter to Vicinia

Silena, a simpleton, daughter to Stellio

Rixula, a serving-girl to Prisius, whose daughter is Livia

MALE CHARACTERS

Memphio, a rich old man, father of Accius

Stellio, an old and wealthy husbandman, father of Silena

Prisius, a fuller, an old man of modest means, father of Livia. A fuller fulls cloth: A fuller cleans wool in a fulling mill.

Sperantus, a farmer, an old man of modest means, father of Candius

Maestius, son to Vicinia

Candius, son to Sperantus, in love with Livia

Accius, a simpleton, son to Memphio

Dromio, a boy, servant to Memphio

Risio, a boy, servant to Stellio

Lucio, a boy, servant to Prisius

Halfpenny, a boy, servant to Sperantus

MINOR CHARACTERS

Synus, a fiddler

Nasutis, a fiddler

Bedunenus, a fiddler

Hackneyman

Sergeant

Scrivener

SCENE:

1

A street in Rochester, Kent, England. On the street are the houses of Memphio, Stellio, Prisius, Sperantus, and Mother Bombie. Also on the street are a scrivener's shop and a tavern.

NOTES:

This play is greatly influenced by Roman comedies in which tricky slaves outwit their masters and earn their freedom. The four serving-boys are bondmen, which means they are in bondage. The word "bondman" can mean serf or slave.

In this society, a person of higher rank would use "thou," "thee," "thine," and "thy" when referring to a person of lower rank. (These terms were also used affectionately and between equals.) A person of lower rank would use "you" and "your" when referring to a person of higher rank.

The word "wench" at this time was not necessarily negative. It was often used affectionately.

The word "mistress" at this time can mean simply a woman who is loved. It can also mean a female head of household.

The word "fair" can mean attractive, beautiful, handsome, and good-looking.

"Sirrah" was a title used to address someone of a social rank inferior to the speaker. Friends, however, could use it to refer to each other, and fathers could call their sons "sirrah."

The verb "cozened" means "tricked" and "cheated."

EDITIONS:

Lyly, John. *The Complete Plays of John Lyly*. Edited by R. Warwick Bond. Oxford: At the Clarendon Press, 1973.

Lyly, John. *Mother Bombie*. Ed. Leah Scragg. The Revels Plays. Manchester and New York: Manchester University Press, 2010.

Lyly, John. *The Plays of John Lyly*. Carter A. Daniel, editor. Lewisburg: Bucknell University Press. London and Toronto: Associated University Presses. 1988.

An online edition (NOT modern spelling) is here:

https://americanshakespearecenter.com/events/
mother-bombie-2015/

I was unable to find and use this edition:

John Lyly's 'Mother Bombie': A Critical Edition. Edited by Harriette A. Andreadis. Renaissance Studies 35. Published 1975. (And published earlier.)

CHAPTER 1

— 1.1 —

Memphio, a wealthy old man, and Dromio, his serving-boy, talked together. They talked mostly about Memphio's son: Accius.

Memphio complained, "Boy, three things make my life miserable: a threadbare purse, a curst wife, and a foolish heir."

A threadbare purse is a threadbare container for money. Memphio was complaining about a lack of money, although he was, in fact, wealthy. In this society, both men and women used what were called purses.

A curst wife is a shrewish wife.

Dromio advised:

"Why, then, sir, there are three medicines for these three maladies: a pike-staff weapon to steal a purse on the highway, a wand of holly to brush choler — anger — from my mistress' tongue, and a young wench for my young master.

"Since your worship, who is wise, begot a fool, so he, who is a fool, may tread out — that is, beget — a wise man."

A proverb stated: A wise man commonly has a fool to his heir.

Memphio replied, "Aye, but Dromio, these medicines bite hot on great evils, for if I do these actions, I might have a rope about my neck, horns upon my head, and in my house a litter of fools."

If he became a highwayman, he could end up being hung.

If he used a holly branch to beat his wife, she could cuckold him to get revenge. A cuckold is a man with an unfaithful wife. In this society, people joked that cuckolds had invisible horns growing on their head.

If he got his foolish son a wench to make pregnant, his home could soon become filled with foolish children.

"Then, sir, you had best let some wise man sit on your son, to hatch him a good wit," Dromio said. "They say, if ravens sit on hens' eggs, the chickens will be black, and so forth."

One problem with proverbs and old sayings is that they can be contradictory. The proverb about ravens and black chickens states that children will be like their parents. That is the opposite of the previous proverb: A wise man commonly has a fool to his heir.

"Why, boy, my son is out of the shell and is grown up, and he has grown a pretty cock," Memphio said.

Hmm. He has grown up to be a handsome man, and he has grown a handsome penis.

Dromio advised, "Carve him, master, and make him a capon, else all your breed — your descendants — will prove coxcombs."

A capon is a castrated cock, aka rooster.

A coxcomb is a fool; professional Fools sometimes wore hats that resembled a cock's comb.

Of course, professional Fools were not fools; professional Fools were often quite wise.

"I marvel that my son is such an ass," Memphio said. "He did not get that from his father."

"He may for any thing you know," Dromio said.

"Why, villain, do thou think that I am a fool?" Memphio asked.

"O no, sir," Dromio said. "Neither are you sure that you are his father."

In the days before DNA analysis, fatherhood could be difficult to prove.

"Rascal, do thou imagine thy mistress has been wicked with her body?" Memphio asked.

"No, but I think she is fantastical of her mind, and it may be, that when this boy was begotten, she thought of a fool, and so she conceived a fool, yourself being very wise, and she surpassingly honest and chaste," Dromio said.

"It may be, for I have heard of an Ethiopian, who thinking of a fair picture, brought forth a fair lady, and yet the fair lady was no bastard," Memphio said.

This society regarded white skin as beautiful.

Persina, Queen of Ethiopia, gave birth to a white daughter, Chariclea. Persina explained this by saying that she had been looking at a painting of Perseus and the naked Andromeda, both of whom were white, when Chariclea was conceived. This story appears in Heliodorus' *Aethiopica*.

"You are well read, sir," Dromio said. "Your son may be a bastard and yet legitimate, yourself a cuckold, and yet my mistress virtuous — all this in conceit: in imagination."

"Come, Dromio, it is my grief to have such a son who must inherit my lands," Memphio said.

Dromio said, "He need not be your heir, sir. I'll beg him for a fool."

If an heir were intellectually incompetent, others could petition the court to be the heir's guardian. This would allow them to have the use of the heir's wealth and lands.

"Vile boy, thou would do that to thy young master?" Memphio said.

"Let me have in a device — a trick," Dromio said. "Let me come up with a plan that suits your needs."

"I'll have thy advice, and if it fadge — if it works — thou shall eat until thou shall sweat, thou shall play until thou sleep, and thou shall sleep until thy bones ache," Memphio said.

"Aye, by the Virgin Mary, now you tickle me and excite me," Dromio said. "I am hungry, playful, and sleepy, and all of these at once. I'll break open this head against the wall, but I'll make it bleed good matter. I'll make my head come up with a good plan."

"Then this is how it is: Thou know I have but one son, and he is a fool," Memphio said.

"A monstrous fool," Dromio said.

"I have a wife and she is an arrant — a complete — scold," Memphio said.

"Ah, master, I smell your device," Dromio said. "I smell your plan. It will be excellent."

"Thou cannot know it until I tell it," Memphio said.

"I see it through your brains," Dromio said. "Your hair is so thin and your skull is so transparent that I may sooner see it than hear it."

"Then, boy, thou have a quick wit, and I have a slow tongue, but what is it?" Memphio asked.

"By the Virgin Mary, either you would have your wife's tongue in your son's head, so that he might be a prating and chattering fool, or you would have his brains in her brain pan — her skull — so that she might be a foolish scold," Dromio said.

"Thou dream, Dromio, there is no such matter," Memphio said. "Thou know I have kept them close, so that my neighbors may think that my son is wise and my wife is temperate and mild-mannered because my neighbors have never heard them speak."

"That is well," Dromio said.

"Thou know that Stellio has a good farm and a fair daughter, yes, so fair that she is mewed up — kept inside the home — and she only looks out at the windows, lest she should be stolen away by some roistering courtier," Memphio said.

Stellio was a wealthy farmer, and Silena was his beautiful daughter.

"That is so, sir," Dromio said.

"Now if I could compass — arrange — a marriage match between my son and Stellio's daughter, Silena, by conference of us parents, and without theirs — without my son and his daughter being consulted — I would be blessed, Stellio would be tricked, and thou would be forever set at liberty," Memphio said.

Stellio would be tricked because his son-in-law would be a fool.

"A singular conceit," Dromio said. "An extraordinary idea."

Memphio said:

"Thus much for my son.

"Now for my wife, I would have this kept from her, else I shall not be able to keep my house from smoke, for let it come to one of her ears, and then woe to both of my ears. I would have her go to my house in the country while we conclude this, and once this is done, I don't care if her tongue never stops wagging."

A proverb stated, "Smoke, rain, and a very cursed [shrewish] wife make a man weary of house and life."

Memphio continued:

"If thou can effect and bring about these things, thou shall make thy master happy."

"Think it done, this noddle — this head — of mine shall coin such a new device and plan that you shall have your son married by tomorrow," Dromio said.

"But take heed so that neither the father nor the maiden will speak to my son, for then his folly will mar all," Memphio said.

The maiden was Stellio's daughter: Silena.

"Lay all the care on me," Dromio said. "*Sublevabo te onere*: I will rid you of a fool."

The Latin means: I will lift this burden from you.

"Will thou rid me for a fool?" Memphio, suspicious, asked.

"Will thou rid me for a fool?" can mean "Will you ride me like the fool I am?"

"Tush, don't quarrel," Dromio said.

"Then for the dowry, let it be at least two hundred ducats, and after his death the farm," Memphio said.

"What else?" Dromio asked.

"Then let us go in, so that I may furnish thee with some better counsel, and I may furnish my son with better apparel," Memphio said.

Dromio said:

"Let me alone and leave it to me."

He then whispered to you, the readers:

"I lack only a wag more to be a part of my plan, and then you shall see an exquisite cozenage — an excellent piece of trickery — and you will see that the father is more fool than the son."

A "wag more" is another boy like Dromio: a boy capable of trickery. Dromio then said:

"But listen, sir. I forgot one thing."

"What's that?" Memphio asked.

"*Expellas furca licet, usque recurret,*" Dromio said.

"What's the meaning of that?" Memphio asked.

The Latin means: Although you cast out nature with a pitchfork, it will always return.

"Why, although your son's folly is thrust up with a pair of horns on a fork, yet being natural it will have his course," Dromio said.

In other words: You can try to cast away nature, but if something is natural — intrinsic to one's character — it will out.

In yet other words: You can try to disguise Accius' foolishness and get him married, but his foolishness will become known.

Dromio was saying, in part, that Accius' marriage would probably be unhappy. The fork can be made by a wife's torso and legs, and the horns can be those of a cuckold: a man with an unfaithful wife.

Dromio was also saying, in part, that marriage is not a cure for foolishness. A man who is foolish before marriage is likely to continue to be foolish after marriage.

According to the *Oxford English Dictionary*, one now-obsolete meaning of the adjective "natural" is an environment "naturally adapted *for*, or applicable *to*, something."

Accius may not be a born fool (the meaning of the noun "natural"), but he may have been raised in an environment that resulted in spoiling him and making him foolish.

Dromio seems to regard Accius as a born fool, but readers will have to form their own opinion.

"I ask thee to say no more, but to go about your plan," Memphio said.

They exited into Memphio's house.

— 1.2 —

Stellio and his serving-boy, Risio, talked together.

Stellio was a wealthy man and the father of Silena.

Stellio said, "Risio, my daughter is surpassingly amiable, but very simple."

"Amiable" means "worthy of being loved." It means both 1) lovable, and 2) lovely.

Risio said, "You mean that she is a fool, sir."

"Indeed, I did imply as much," Stellio said.

"Then I apply her characteristics fittingly: the one characteristic she takes from her father, the other characteristic she takes from her mother, and so now you may be sure she is your own," Risio said.

Hmm. Deliberately ambiguous, that. Is it from the father or from the mother that she gets her foolishness? From the other parent (but which one is that?), she gets her good looks.

Stellio said:

"I have penned her up and enclosed her in a chamber, having only a window to look out, so that youths, seeing her fair cheeks, may be enamored before they hear her fond, foolish speech.

"How do thou like this head?"

Stellio was referring to his problem-solving: He kept his daughter at home where youths could see her beauty but not talk to her and discover her foolishness.

Risio said, "There is very good workmanship in it, but the matter is only base. If the stuff — the filling — had been as good as the mold, your daughter would have been as wise as she is beautiful."

Risio was commenting on Stellio's head: his appearance and his intellect. Yes, Stellio was good-looking, but according to Risio, Stellio was somewhat lacking in his brain.

"Do thou think she took her foolishness from me?" Stellio asked.

Risio said, "Aye, and so cunningly, that she took it not from you."

In other words: She got her foolishness from you, but although she took it from you, you are still foolish.

"Well, *Quod natura dedit tollere nemo potest*," Stellio said.

The Latin means: No man can take away what came from nature.

Risio said, "That is a good piece of evidence to prove the fee-simple of your daughter's folly."

"Why?" Stellio asked.

Risio said, "It came by nature, and if none can take it away, it is perpetual."

Property that is owned in fee-simple is absolute ownership. The property belongs to the owner, and it can be passed down to his heirs. Risio was saying that the foolishness of Stellio has been passed down to his daughter.

Stellio said:

"No, Risio, she is no natural fool. She was not born a fool.

"Her simplicity and foolishness consist in these things:

"She thinks that she is a subtle thinker, but she is not.

"When she is rude, she imagines that she is courtly and sophisticated.

"Because of this over-esteeming her abilities, she has overweening pride."

"Well, what follows?" Risio asked.

Stellio said:

"Risio, this is my plot. Memphio has a pretty stripling — a good-looking youth named Accius — who is his son, whom with overindulgence he has spoiled and made wanton: The boy's girdle — that is, his sash — must be warmed, the air must not breathe on him, he must lie in bed until noon, and yet in his bed he must break his fast."

Accius may not be a born fool; his foolishness may be a result of his being spoiled.

Stellio continued:

"Those things that I do to conceal the folly of my daughter, that he does in too much spoiling and pampering of his son."

Memphio's too much spoiling and pampering of his son, Accius, kept Accius at home.

Stellio continued:

"Now, Risio, how shall I compass — that is, arrange — a marriage match between my girl and his boy?"

"Why, with a pair of compasses," Risio said. "If thou bring them both into the circle, I'll guarantee they'll match themselves."

A compass is a mechanical device used to draw circles.

"Tush, plot it for me so that without ever speaking one to another, they will fall in love with each other," Stellio said. "I don't like solemn wooing, it is for courtiers, let country folks believe others' reports and gossips as much as their own opinions."

Risio said, "O, then as long as it is a marriage match, you don't care how it comes about."

Stellio said, "No, I don't care, and I would not care for a marriage match either, if I weren't thirsting after my neighbor's farm."

Risio said to himself, sarcastically:

"A very good nature."

He then said out loud:

"Well, if by flat wit and my ingenuity, I bring this to pass, what's my reward?"

"Whatsoever thou will ask," Stellio said.

"I'll ask for no more than by my wit I can get in the bargain," Risio said.

"Then get on about it," Stellio said.

He exited into his house.

Risio said to himself about Stellio:

"If I come not about — that is, if I don't outsmart you — never trust me."

He added:

"I'll seek out Dromio, the counselor of my conceit. He can advise me about a plot that will get me what I want."

— 1.3 —

Prisius and Sperantus talked together.

Prisius was a fuller, a man of modest means, and the father of Livia.

Sperantus was a farmer, a man of modest means, and the father of Candius.

Prisius said, "It is unneighborly done to allow your son since he came from the university to spend his time in seeking love, and unwisely done to let him hover over my daughter, who has nothing for her dowry except her needle, and must prove to be a sempster: a seamstress. Nor does he have anything to take to except a grammar book, and he cannot at the best be anything except a schoolmaster."

One way to advance in life is to marry someone with means. Candius and Livia were in love, but their parents had only modest means. Both of their fathers wanted them to marry someone of more-than-modest means.

Sperantus said:

"Prisius, you bite and whine, you wring me on the withers, and yet you winch yourself."

An ill-fitting saddle will hurt a horse by wringing it on the withers: the highest part of the back of the horse.

A proverb stated, "Touch a galled horse on the back, and he will wince."

Sperantus continued:

"It is you who go about to match your girl with my boy. She is more fit for sewing seams than for marriage, and he is more fit for a rod than a wife."

"Her birth requires a better bridegroom than such a groom," Prisius said.

A groom is lower-class; a groom can be a servant.

"And his bringing up requires another gate marriage than such a minion," Sperantus said.

"Another gate marriage" is "a different kind of marriage."

A minion can be a hussy.

"Marry gup!" Prisius said. "I am sure he has no better bread than is made of wheat, nor has he worn finer cloth than is made of wool, nor has he learned better manners than are taught in schools."

Prisius was saying that Sperantus' son was not a gentleman.

"Marry gup" means "Bah!"

To "eat better bread than is made of wheat" is to "have extremely fastidious tastes."

In this society, sumptuary laws stated what kind of clothing each social class could wear. Wool was worn by the lower class.

Excellent manners were associated with the court, not with the university.

Sperantus said, "Nor does your minx have no better grandfather than a tailor, who (as I have heard) was poor and proud. Nor has she a better father than yourself, unless your wife borrowed a better man to make her daughter a gentlewoman."

The "better man" would make Prisius a cuckold.

Prisius said, "Don't twit — insult — me with my ancestors, nor my wife's honesty and chastity. If thou do —"

He threatened Sperantus.

"Thou had best hold thy hands still, and yet it is impossible now I remember, for thou have the palsy and your hands shake," Sperantus said.

"My hands shake so much that if thou were in an appropriate place, there I would teach thee to cog," Prisius said.

To "cog" can mean to lie. This is the meaning Prisius meant.

He would beat up Sperantus and thereby show that Sperantus was lying about Prisius' hands shaking.

To "cog" can also mean to cheat, as with tricky throws of the dice. Sperantus now used this meaning.

Sperantus said:

"Nay, if thy hands shake, I guarantee that thou cannot teach anyone to cog.

"But neighbor, let not two old fools fall out for two young wantons."

The wantons were their children, both of whom were wayward, according to their fathers.

Prisius said, "Indeed, it becomes men of our experience to reason, not rail: to debate the matter, not to combat it."

Sperantus said:

"Well, then I'll tell thee this in a friendly manner.

"I have almost these two years cast in my head and deliberated about how I might match my princox — my saucy son — with Stellio's daughter, Silena, whom I have heard to be very fair, and whom I know shall be very rich. She is his heir, he dotes on her, he is old and stoops with his age, and he shortly must die, yet by no means, either by blessing or cursing, can I win my son to be a wooer, which I know proceeds not from bashfulness but stubbornness, for he knows his good although I am the one who says it — he has wit at will."

Sperantus' son, Candius, understood courteous behavior, and he had intellectual gifts.

"As for his personage, I don't care who sees him. I can tell you he is able to make a lady's mouth water if she does not close her eyes."

Candius was a handsome young man.

Prisius responded:

"Stop, Sperantus, this is like my case, for I have been tampering and scheming as long as you have to have a marriage committed and arranged between my wench and Memphio's only son: Accius.

"They say that he is as goodly and splendid a youth as one shall see in a summer's day, and as neat and trim a stripling as ever went on neat's leather."

Neat's leather is cowhide. Accius walks on leather-soled shoes.

Prisius continued:

"His father will not let him be out of his sight — he is so tender over him. He — the son — still sleeps with his mother for fear of catching cold.

"Now my pretty but wayward elf — my daughter Livia — is as proud as the day is long, and she will have none of him. She, forsooth, will choose her own husband. She thinks that made marriages — arranged marriages — prove to be mad marriages! She will choose with her eye and like with her heart before she will consent with her tongue. Neither father nor mother, kith nor kin — countrymen or blood relatives — shall be her carver in a husband."

The head of the household carved the meat at the dinner table. Livia wanted to metaphorically carve her own meat: to choose her own husband.

Prisius continued:

"She will fall, too, where she likes best."

She would metaphorically fall to the meal: She would satisfy her desires with and fall in bed with the man she herself would choose to be her husband.

Prisius continued:

"And thus the chick that is scarcely out of the shell cackles as though she had been trodden with — used by — a hundred cocks and had been mother of a thousand eggs."

Livia was a young woman who wanted to choose her own mate. According to her father, who wanted to choose her husband for her, that made her headstrong.

Sperantus said, "Well, then, this is our best course of action, seeing we know each other's mind: to devise a way to govern our own children. As for my boy, I'll keep him to his books, and study shall make him cease to love your daughter. I'll break him of his will, or I'll break his bones with a cudgel."

Prisius said:

"And I'll no more dandle — that is, indulge, my daughter. She shall prick on a cloth — sew — until her fingers ache. If she doesn't, I'll give her permission to make my heart ache."

He saw Candius and Livia walking toward them, although they did not see Sperantus and him.

Prisius then said:

"But in good time — at an appropriate moment, although with ill luck — look! Both of them are together. Let us stand nearby and conceal ourselves and hear everything. By doing that, we shall prevent all that we don't like."

The two fathers hid themselves.

Candius and Livia entered the scene. Candius was carrying a book, and Livia was holding a sampler.

Sperantus whispered, "This happens at an opportune time. Be careful that you don't cough, Prisius."

Prisius whispered, "Bah. Don't you spit, and I'll guarantee that my beard is as good as a handkerchief for stopping a cough."

Livia said, "Sweet Candius, if thy father should see us alone, wouldn't he fret? I think that the old man should be full of fumes."

He would fume with anger: His brain would be filled with noxious thoughts.

Candius said, "Bah, let him fret one heartstring against another — he shall never trouble the least vein of my little finger. The churlish old man thinks that no one is wise unless he has a beard that hangs dangling to his waist. When my face is as plastered with hair as is his, then perhaps my understanding may stumble on his staidness."

If Candius' understanding were to become as staid as the understanding of Livia's father, that would be equivalent to a stumble. That is not something to be wished for.

Prisius, the father of Livia, whispered, "Aye? In what book did you read that lesson? Where did you learn that?"

Sperantus, the father of Candius, whispered, "I don't know in what book he read it, but I am sure he was a knave to learn it."

Candius said, "I believe, fair Livia, if your sour sire were to see you with your sweetheart, he would not be very patient."

Livia said:

"I've taken some care for that: I am prepared.

"I'll ask him for his blessing as my father, but I'll never take his counsel and advice about a husband. There is as much difference between my golden thoughts and his leaden advice, as there is between his silver hairs and my amber locks. I know he will cough for anger that I don't yield to his wishes, but he shall cough me a fool — that is, make a fool of himself — for his labor."

Sperantus whispered to Prisius, "Where did your daughter pick that work? Out of broad-stitch?"

In other words: Where did she get that idea?

Something that is "broad" is done without restraint. Livia was not restrained by her father's wishes.

"Picked" means to unpick stitches.

Stitches hold something together. Livia's actions — a metaphorical unpicking of stitches — could separate her from her father.

Prisius whispered, "Out of a flirt's sampler, but let us stay until the end. This is just the beginning; you shall hear two children 'well brought up.'"

A sampler is a piece of work that illustrates the sewer's skill.

Candius said:

"Parents in these days have grown peevish and perverse. They rock their children in their cradles until they sleep, and then they cross them about their bridals until their hearts ache. Marriage among them has become a market: What dowry will you give with your daughter? What jointure will you make for your son?"

A jointure is property held in common between a husband and a wife. After the husband dies, the property is used to support the widow.

"And many a match is broken off for a penny more or less, as though they could not afford their children at such a price, when nothing should cheapen such ware — that is, should ask a price for a spouse — except affection, and nothing should buy it except love."

"Learnedly and like a scholar," Sperantus whispered sarcastically.

Livia said:

"Indeed, our parents take great care to make us ask blessing and say grace when we are little ones, and when we grow up to the years of judgment, they deprive us of the greatest blessing, and the most gracious things to our minds, the liberty of our minds: They give us pap — soft baby food — with a spoon before we can speak, and when we speak for that which we love, they give us pap with a hatchet."

"Pap with a hatchet" is "bad treatment with a veneer of kindness."

Livia continued:

"Because their fancies have grown musty with hoary — grey — old age, nothing that has the flavor of sweet youth can therefore taste good in their thoughts. They study twenty years together to make us grow as straight as a wand, and in the end by bowing us make us as crooked as a cammock."

A "cammock" is a twisted branch that can be trimmed and used as a cane.

Livia continued:

"For my own part, sweet Candius, they shall pardon me — I will not obey them — for I will measure my love by my own judgment, not by my father's purse nor by his peevishness. Nature has made me his child, not his slave. I would hate Memphio and his son in a deadly way, if I thought his son would place his affection by his father's appointment."

Memphio's son was Accius. Livia would hate Accius if he would fall in love with whomever Memphio told him to fall in love.

"Wittily but uncivilly," Prisius whispered.

Livia had spoken cleverly but without conventional obedience to her father.

Candius said:

"Be of that mind always, my fair Livia. Let our fathers lay their purses together; we will lay our hearts together. I will never woo where I cannot love — let Stellio enjoy his daughter."

"Enjoy" refers to the joy a couple find in bed together. Candius was saying that Stellio might as well marry his daughter, Silena, because he, Candius, would not.

Candius then asked:

"But what have you wrought here in this sampler?"

Livia said:

"Flowers, fowls, beasts, fishes, trees, plants, stones, and what not.

"Among flowers, Cowslips and Lilies for our names Candius and Livia.

"Among fowl, turtledoves and sparrows, for our truth and desires."

Turtledoves are associated with loyalty in love, and sparrows are associated with sexual desire.

Livia continued:

"Among beasts, the fox and the ermine for policy and beauty."

Foxes are associated with cunning, and ermines have a beautiful winter coat.

Livia continued:

"Among fishes, the cockle and the tortoise, because of Venus."

Venus was born off the coast of Cyprus, and she was depicted standing on a cockle (scallop) shell in a painting by Botticelli.

She is sometimes depicted with a foot on a tortoise. Tortoises are associated with staying at home because they carry their homes on their back.

Livia continued:

"Among trees, the vine wreathing about the elm for our embracings.

"Among stones, abeston, which after it becomes hot will never be cold, for our constancies.

"Among plants, thyme and heart's-ease, to note that if we take time, we shall ease our hearts."

"There's a girl who knows her lerripoop," Prisius whispered.

Literally, a lerripoop is the long tail of a university graduate's academic hood. Figuratively, it is a lesson.

"Listen and you shall hear my son's learning," Sperantus said, seeing Livia looking at the book that Candius was holding.

"What book is that?" Livia asked.

Candius said, "It is by a fine, pleasant poet, a poet who entreats of the art of Love, and of the remedy for Love."

The poet is Ovid, author of *Ars Amatoria*: *The Art of Love*.

"Is there art in love?" Livia asked.

Candius said, "It is a short art and a certain art. There are three rules in three lines."

"Please repeat them," Livia requested.

Candius quoted from memory or read out loud:

"*Principio, quod amare velis, reperire labora, [...]*

"*Proximus huic labor est placidam exorare puellam.*

"*Tertius, ut longo tempore duret amor.*"

The Latin lines came from Ovid's *Arts Amatoria*, Book 1, lines 35, 37-38.

Translated, they are:

"First, find someone to love. [...]

"Next, win the one you want to love you.

"Third, make love long lasting."

Livia said, "I am no Latinist, Candius. You must construe — translate — it."

Candius said:

"So I will and parse it, too: Thou shall be acquainted with case, gender, and number.

"First, one must find out a mistress — a woman to love — whom before all others he vows to serve.

"Secondly, he shall use all the means that he may to obtain her.

"And finally, he must study and work to keep her with deserts, faith, and secrecy."

"What's the remedy?" Livia asked.

"Death," Candius said.

Death "cures" love.

"What of all the book is the conclusion?" Livia asked.

Candius answered, "This one verse: *Non caret essertu quod voluere duo.*"

The Latin means: What two people have willed does not lack accomplishment.

In other words: When two people agree to do something, that something will be accomplished.

"What's that?" Livia asked.

Candius answered, "Where two are agreed, it is impossible for anything except that they must speed — they must succeed."

Livia said, "Then we cannot fail; therefore, give me thy hand, Candius."

They could become engaged right now. A betrothal occurred when a man and a woman held hands and pledged to marry each other.

Prisius stepped into the open and said, "Wait, Livia, take me with you. Let's understand each other. A betrothal is not good in law without witness."

Sperantus stepped into the open and said, "And as I remember, there must be two witnesses to a betrothal. May God give you joy, Candius. I was worth the bidding to the dinner, although not worthy to be of the counsel."

Sperantus had not been asked to give his advice about whom Candius should marry and so he was not supposed to witness the engagement, but if the wedding were held, he would be invited to a celebratory meal.

"I think this hot love has provided but cold cheer," Prisius said.

"Cheer" is 1) food, and 2) a cheerful state of mind.

"Cold cheer" is 1) cold food, aka a bad meal, and 2) a joyless state of mind.

Sperantus said, "Bah, to be in love is no lack, but don't blush, Candius. You need not be ashamed of your cunning and learning. You have made love a book case — a subject of study — and you have spent your time well at the university, learning to love by art, and learning to hate against nature, but I perceive, the worser child is the better lover."

"Hate against nature" means "hate (disobey) your own father."

Prisius said:

"And my minion — my daughter the hussy — has wrought well, where every stitch in her sampler is a pricking stitch at my heart.

"You take your pleasure by criticizing parents: They are peevish fools, churls, and miserable old men, and they are overgrown with ignorance, because they are overworn with age.

"Little shall thou know what it is to be a father before thyself will be a mother, when thou shall breed thy child with continual pains, and bringing it forth with deadly pangs, nurse it with thine own paps [breasts], and nourish it up with motherly tenderness, and then find that they curse thee with their hearts, when they should ask blessing on their knees, and the collop — the offspring — of thine own bowels will be the torture of thine own soul.

"With tears trickling down thy cheeks, and with drops of blood falling from thy heart, thou will in uttering thy mind wish them rather unborn than unnatural and disobedient to their parents, and thou will wish to have had their cradles be their graves rather than to have thy death be their bridals."

Their bridals — their celebratory betrothals and weddings — will be the death of their parents. So said Prisius.

Prisius continued:

"But I will not dispute what thou should have done, although I will correct what thou have done. I perceive sewing is an idle, unprofitable exercise, and I perceive that every day there come more thoughts into thine head than stitches into thy work. I'll see whether you can spin a better mind than you have stitched, and if I don't coop you up, then let me be the capon."

Prisius wanted to lock up his daughter and not allow her to see Candius. If Prisius did not do that, then let him — Prisius — be castrated like a capon. So said Prisius.

Sperantus said to his son:

"As for you, sir boy, instead of poring on a book, you shall hold the plow. I'll make repentance reap what wantonness has sown, but we are both well served: The sons must be the masters, and the fathers must be the old, incapacitated gaffers. What we fathers get together with a rake, our sons cast abroad with a pitchfork, and we fathers must weary our legs to purchase our children coats of arms.

"Well, seeing that booking — academic study — is but idleness, I'll see whether threshing is any occupation. Thy mind shall stoop to my fortune, or my mind shall break the laws of nature."

Sperantus' fortune was his lot in life. He was a farmer, and he was threatening to make his son a farmer instead of an academic.

According to Sperantus, the laws of nature included filial piety: the son must obey the father. If the son did not do that, then Sperantus would himself break the laws of nature: He would not fulfill one or more obligations of the father to the son.

Sperantus continued:

"How like a micher — a truant — he stands, as though he had truanted from honesty."

He said to his son:

"Get thee in, and as for the rest, leave it to me.

"Get in, villain!"

Prisius said to his daughter:

"And you, pretty minx, who must be fed with love upon sops, I'll take an order — I'll make arrangements — to cram you with sorrows."

A sop is a cake soaked in wine. In this case, it is a delicacy given to a bride.

Prisius continued:

"Get inside without making nasty looks or replies."

Candius and Livia exited, each into the house of his or her father.

Sperantus said:

"Let us follow after them.

"If you deal as rigorously with yours as I will with mine, you shall see that hot love will wax — grow — soon cold.

"I'll tame the proud boy, and I'll send him as far from his love as he is from his duty."

Prisius said, "Let us go about it, and let us also go on with matching them according to our minds. It was fortunate that we prevented that betrothal by chance, which we could never have suspected they would do by the circumstantial evidence available to us."

They exited.

CHAPTER 2
— 2.1 —

Dromio and Risio walked toward each other. Neither saw the other at first.

Dromio was a serving-boy to Memphio, and Risio was a serving-boy to Stellio.

Memphio was the father of Accius, and Stellio was the father of Silena.

Accius and Silena were simpletons.

Dromio said to himself, "Now if I could meet with Risio, it would be a world of waggery. People would marvel at our mischief."

Risio said to himself, "Oh, I wish that it would be my luck *obviam dare Dromio* — to stumble upon Dromio — on whom I do nothing but dream."

Dromio said to himself, "Risio's knavery and my wit and intelligence would make our masters, who are wise, fools; would make their children, who are fools, beggars; and would make Risio and me, who are bondmen, free."

Seeing Dromio, Risio said to himself, "With Dromio to cheat, and with me to conjure up a plan, we would make such alterations that our masters would serve themselves and be their own servants, the idiots their children would serve us, and we would wake our wits and put our brains to work among them all."

Seeing Risio, Dromio said to himself:

"*Hem quam opportune!* — Well, how opportune!

"Look and see if he has not dropped full in my dish."

Risio said to himself, "*Lupus in fabula!*"

The Latin means: The wolf in the story. The expression refers to a person who is being gossiped about suddenly showing up in the midst of the gossip.

"Dromio, embrace me, hug me, and kiss my hand, for I must make thee fortunate," Risio said.

Risio wanted Dromio to treat him as a friend who had done him a favor.

"Risio, honor me, kneel down to me, and kiss my feet, for I must make thee blessed," Dromio said.

Dromio wanted Risio to treat him as a priest who had conferred some important blessing on him.

"My master, old Stellio, has a fool as his daughter," Risio said.

"My master, old Memphio, has a fool as his son," Dromio said.

"I must convey a contract," Risio said.

"And I must convey a contract," Dromio said.

The contract was a marriage contract between the simpletons Accius and Silena. Risio and Dromio were supposed to arrange the same marriage.

"This contract is between her and Memphio's son without one of them speaking to the other," Risio said.

"This contract is between him and Stellio's daughter without one of them speaking to the other," Dromio said.

The fathers of these simpletons did not want them to talk to each other because each simpleton would discover the other simpleton's foolishness.

"Do thou mock me, Dromio?" Risio asked.

"Or thou are mocking me," Dromio said.

"Not I, for all this is true," Risio said.

"And all this is true," Dromio said.

"Then we are both driven to our wits' ends, for if either of them had been wise, we might have tempered — that is, secretly arranged — if no marriage, yet a close marriage," Risio said.

A close marriage is a secret marriage: one not publicly celebrated.

"Well, let us sharpen our accounts, for there's no better grindstone for a young man's head than to have it whet upon an old man's purse," Dromio said. "Oh, thou shall see my knavery shave like a razor!"

His words used the imagery of a knife being sharpened on a whetstone.

Dromio wanted to take advantage of his master: Memphio.

Risio said, "Thou for the edge, and I for the point will make the fool bestride our mistress' backs, and then have at the bag with the dudgeon haft — that is, with the dudgeon dagger, by which hangs his tantony pouch."

Weapons have edges and points, but the serving-boys' main weapons were their wit and intelligence.

The fool is Accius, the mistress [woman they are trying to get married] is Silena, and the "backs" are buttocks.

The two serving-boys could arrange the requested marriage and then they could use their wits to attempt to get money from the two old fathers of the couple.

Dudgeon is a wood used for the handles of good knives.

"Tantony" is an abbreviation of St. Anthony of Abbot, patron saint of animals, including pigs. A tantony pouch may be a purse made out of pigskin.

Literally, Risio was talking about using a knife to cut the strings of a purse (moneybag) hanging from a belt. Cutpurses — pickpockets — did this.

Hmm. Figuratively, much bawdiness is in this passage. The dagger is a penis, and the pouch refers to a scrotum.

The "bag" is "baggage": Silena. One meaning of "baggage" is "strumpet."

Risio wanted to get Silena married off, and then he wanted to take advantage of his master: Stellio.

"These old huddles — old men — have such strong purses with locks that when they shut them, they go off like a snaphance," Dromio said.

A snaphance is a flint-and-hammer mechanism used in early pistols.

Risio said:

The old fashion is best, a purse with a ring round about it, as a circle to course — chase — a knave's hand from it."

An old-fashioned purse is a moneybag with a drawstring to keep the circle — the opening — closed and to try to prevent thievery. The moneybag was hung from a belt.

If this passage is meant to be bawdy, the circle would be the opening of a vagina.

Of course, once a reader realizes just how bawdy the Elizabethan playwrights were in their plays, it becomes possible to see bawdiness where it is not intended.

Risio continued:

"But Dromio, they say that two people may keep counsel — a secret — if one is away, but to convey — to carry out — knavery, two are too few, and four are too many."

Hmm. There are four serving-boys in Lyly's play: Dromio, Risio, Halfpenny, and Lucio. All of them engage in knavery together.

Seeing someone coming toward them, Dromio said, "And in good time, look where Halfpenny, Sperantus' serving-boy, comes. Although he is bound up in decimo sexto for carriage, yet he is a wit in folio for cozenage and cheating."

Halfpenny was small: A decimo sexto is a book whose pages are made from paper folded four times to produce sixteen small pages.

But Halfpenny's ability to cheat others was large: A folio is a book whose pages are made from paper folded only once.

Halfpenny was a serving-boy to Sperantus, who was the father of Candius, who was in love with Livia, who was the daughter of Prisius.

Halfpenny entered the scene.

Dromio then said:

"Single Halfpenny, what news are now current?"

Being small, Halfpenny is Single Halfpenny. He is half the size of two Halfpennies.

Current news is new news as opposed to old news.

Current coinage is legal coinage as opposed to counterfeit currency.

Halfpenny replied, "Nothing but that such double coistrels as you are, are counterfeit!"

"Coistrels" are scoundrels.

"Double" can mean 1) two, and 2) cheat.

Halfpenny knows that Dromio and Risio are two cheating scoundrels. Halfpenny himself is a cheating scoundrel.

"As you are so dapper — so smart — we'll send you for a Halfpenny loaf," Risio said.

They would send Halfpenny on an errand that he would not return from, as he would be exchanged for the bread.

"I shall go for silver, though, when you shall be nailed up for slips," Halfpenny said.

Slips are counterfeit coins. Tradesmen nailed them to their counters or walls: This kept them out of circulation and probably decreased the number of people deliberately attempting to use counterfeit coins at these places.

Halfpenny would be recognized as being of value: silver. But Dromio and Risio would be recognized as worthless: counterfeits.

"Thou are a slipstring, I'll warrant," Dromio said.

A slipstring is something such as a dog that has slipped from a leash.

"I hope you shall never slip string, but hang steady," Halfpenny said.

A kind of string is a noose. Halfpenny was saying that he hoped that Dromio would not escape from the noose.

"Dromio, look here, now is my hand on my Halfpenny," Risio said, taking hold of Halfpenny.

A proverb stated, "I will lay my hand on my halfpenny ere [before] I part with it."

Halfpenny said, "Thou lie, thou have not a farthing to lay thy hands on — I am none of thine. But let me be wagging — be going on my way — my head is full of hammers, and they have so malleted — beaten — my wit that I am almost a malcontent."

A head full of hammers is a brain working at full speed.

"Why, what's the matter?" Dromio asked.

Halfpenny said, "My master has a fine scholar as his son, and Prisius has a fair lass as his daughter."

Halfpenny's master was Sperantus, who was the father of Candius, who was in love with Livia, who was the daughter of Prisius.

"Well," Dromio said.

"The two — Candius and Livia — love one another deadly: almost to the point of death," Halfpenny said.

"In good time," Risio said. "Very well."

Halfpenny said, "The fathers have put them up and shut them away, utterly disliking the match, and they have appointed that the one shall have Memphio's son, and the other shall have Stellio's daughter."

Sperantus wanted his son, Candius, to marry Stellio's daughter, Silena.

Prisius wanted his daughter, Livia, to marry Memphio's son, Accius.

And, of course, Memphio and Stellio wanted their children, Accius and Silena, to marry each other.

Accius and Silena were alike in that they were simpletons.

Halfpenny continued:

"This works like wax, but how it will fadge — work out — in the end, the hen that sits next to the cock cannot tell."

Something that "works like wax" is easily done. Wax is easily heated and manipulated.

Risio said to Halfpenny, "If thou have just any spice of knavery, we'll make thee happy."

Halfpenny said, "Bah, don't doubt that I am as full for my pitch — size — as you are for yours. A wren's egg is as full of meat as a goose egg, although there is not as much in it. You shall find this head well stuffed, although little stuff went into it."

A wren's egg is as full of meat as a goose egg if both are 100 percent full.

Halfpenny was small, and so his brain was small, but he was very intelligent.

Dromio said:

"*Laudo ingenium.* I like thy sconce."

The Latin means: I like the way you think.

A "sconce" is a head.

Dromio continued:

"So then listen:

"Memphio made me a part of his plan to marry his son, Accius, to Stellio's daughter.

"Stellio made Risio a part of his plan to marry his daughter, Silena, to Memphio's son.

"To be short, their children — Accius and Silena — are both fools."

Halfpenny, who was short in height, said:

"But they are not fools who are short.

"If I thought thou meant so, *Senties qui vir sim*: Thou should have a crow to pull."

The Latin means: You shall realize what kind of man I am.

They would have a quarrel.

"Have a crow to pull (pluck, pick)" is similar to "have a bone to pick." It is a point to quarrel over.

Risio said:

"Don't be angry, Halfpenny. For fellowship we will all be fools, and for gain we will all be knaves."

Halfpenny laughed.

Risio asked:

"But why do thou laugh?"

"I laugh at my own conceit and quick censure — my own imagination and my own quick judgment," Halfpenny said.

"What's the matter?" Risio asked.

"Suddenly I thought you two were asses, and that the least ass was the more ass," Halfpenny said.

"Thou are a fool," Risio said. "That cannot be."

"Yea, my young master taught me to prove it by learning, and so I can prove it by using a verse out of Ovid," Halfpenny said.

"Please, tell us how," Risio requested.

"You must first for fashion's sake — as a matter of form — confess yourselves to be asses," Halfpenny said.

"Well," Dromio said.

"Then you stand here, and you stand there," Halfpenny said, pointing to the places he Dromio and Risio to stand.

"Get to it," Risio said. "Tell us."

Halfpenny said, "Then this is the verse as I point it: *Cum mala per longas invaluere moras*."

The Latin is derived from Ovid, *Ars Amatoria*, 92. Ovid wrote *convaluere* rather than *invaluere*.

Cum mala per longas invaluere moras means: When you stay ill for a long time.

Cum mala per longas convaluere moras means: When you have a long delay in recovering from an illness.

The meaning of the Latin passage spoken by Halfpenny meaning is not relevant although its sound is.

Halfpenny pointed to the taller — the longer — boy when he said "*longas*."

Halfpenny pointed to the shorter boy when he said "*moras*."

Halfpenny then said, "So you see the least ass is the more ass.

Longas sounds like "long ass."

Moras sounds like "more ass."

The shorter boy is the less tall — least tall — boy. If he is an ass, then he is the least ass. According to Halfpenny's thinking, the least ass is also the more ass.

Halfpenny, however, was the least tall of the three serving-boys.

Risio said:

"We'll bite thee for an ape if thou bob us like asses."

A "bob" is a blow; it is also a trick.

Risio then said:

"But to end all, if thou join with us, we will make a marriage match between the two fools, for that must be our tasks, and thou shall devise to couple Candius and Livia, by over-reaching and out-witting their fathers."

Halfpenny replied:

"Let me alone; leave it to me. *Non enim mea pigra juventus*: There's matter in this noddle."

The Latin means: My youth is not without resources.

A "noddle" is a head.

Lucio entered the scene.

Seeing Lucio, Halfpenny said:

"But look where Prisius' serving-boy is coming, as fit as a pudding for a dog's mouth."

Prisius was the father of Livia, who was in love with Candius.

"Pop three knaves in a sheath," Lucio said. "I'll make it a right Tunbridge case, and I'll be the bodkin."

With "knaves," Lucio was punning on "knives."

A case is a sheath, and Tunbridge is a town in Kent.

A bodkin is a dagger. It is also an awl for boring holes.

With Lucio as a bodkin, the four serving-boys made a full set of knives, or a full set of knaves.

Risio said, "The bodkin is here already, so you must be the knife."

A bodkin is a small knife (or it is an awl), and Halfpenny was the smallest boy among the four serving-boys.

"I am the bodkin," Halfpenny said. "Look well after your ears, for I must bore or bear them."

An Elizabethan punishment was to cut off an offender's ears. In the character of a bodkin, aka small knife, Halfpenny could do that and then carry away the ears.

Another Elizabethan punishment was to make holes in an offender's ears, which could be nailed to a pillory. In the character of a bodkin, aka awl, Halfpenny could do that.

Dromio said, "Shut your mouth. Mew — cage — thy tongue or we'll cut it out. I speak this representing the person of a knife, as thou spoke that in shadow — that is, while playing the part — of a bodkin."

Lucio said, "I must be gone. *Taedet*: It irks me to leave. *Oportet*. It behooves me to leave. My wits work — that is, ferment — like barm, alias yeast, alias sizing, alias rising, alias God's good."

The Latin *taedet* means: He is tired.

The Latin *oportet* means: It is necessary.

"Barm," "sizing," "rising," and "God's good" are all names for yeast, which is used in the making of ale.

Halfpenny said, "The new wine is in thine head, yet he was eager to take this metaphor from ale, and now that you talk about ale, let us all go to the wine. Let us all go to the tavern."

"Four makes a mess, and we have a mess of masters who must be cozened and cheated, so let us lay our heads together," Dromio said. "They are married and cannot."

In this society, people joked that cuckolds — men with unfaithful wives — had invisible horns growing on their head. Because of the horns, the four masters could not lay their heads together.

Halfpenny said:

"Let us consult at the tavern, where after we drink to the health of Memphio, we will drink to the life of Stellio, I will carouse — drink —

to Prisius, and you, Lucio, will brinch — propose a toast — to Mas, aka Master, Sperantus."

Neither Halfpenny nor Lucio would propose a toast to his own master, but each would drink to the other serving-boy's master.

Halfpenny then said:

"We shall cast our accounts and discharge our stomachs, like men who can digest anything."

"Digest" can mean 1) consume, and 2) plot.

"Cast" means 1) calculate, and 2) vomit. The serving-boys would vomit the ale they had paid for and had drunk.

"I don't see yet what you go about — what you are plotting," Lucio said.

Dromio said:

"Lucio, who can pierce a mud wall that is twenty-foot thick, would make us believe that he cannot see a candle through a paper lantern.

"His knavery is beyond *ela*, and yet he says he doesn't know *gam ut*."

Ela is the highest note in the hexachord scale, and *gam ut* is the lowest note in the hexachord scale.

"I am ready, if any cozenage and cheating is ripe," Lucio said. "I'll shake the tree."

Halfpenny said, "I hope to see thee so strong that you shake three trees at once."

These are the serving-boys' three plots:

Getting Candius and Livia married.

Getting Accius to agree to marry Silena.

Getting Silena to agree to marry Accius.

Dromio said, "We burn and waste time, for I must give a reckoning of my day's work. Let us get close to the bush *ad deliberandum* — to deliberate."

The bush is the tavern, which displayed an ivy branch or had an ivy bush as a sign that it served ale. Bacchus, god of wine, wears a wreath made of ivy, which is sacred to him.

Halfpenny said, "Indeed, *inter pocula philosophundum* — to philosophize among the cups. It is good to plead — to debate — among pots."

Risio said, "Thine situation will be the worst. I fear we shall leave a Halfpenny in hand."

A proverb stated, "He drank till he gave up his halfpenny."

The proverb refers to getting drunk.

Risio was joking that Halfpenny would get drunk and have to be left behind.

Halfpenny said, "Why, say thou that thou have left a print deeper in thy hand already than a halfpenny can leave, unless it should singe worse than a hot iron."

Some offenders were branded on the hand. Halfpenny was saying that Risio was a branded criminal.

"We are all friends, and so let us sing," Lucio said. "It is a pleasant thing to go into the tavern, clearing the throat."

All sang:

"*Iô [Hail], Bacchus! To thy table.*

"*Thou call every drunken rabble,*

"*We already are stiff [hard] drinkers,*

"*[So] Then seal us for thy jolly skinkers [bartenders].*"

Dromio sang:

"*Wine, O wine!*

"*O juice divine!*

"*How do thou the noll [head, or drunkard] refine!*"

Risio sang:

"*Plump thou make men's ruby faces,*

"*And from girls can fetch embraces.*"

Halfpenny sang:

"*By thee our noses swell,*

"*With sparkling carbuncle.*"

A carbuncle is 1) literally, a fiery red gem, and 2) figuratively, the red of an alcoholic's face.

Lucio sang:

"*Oh, the dear blood of grapes,*

"*Turns us to antic [grotesque] shapes,*

"*Now to show tricks like apes.*"

Dromio sang:

"*Now lion-like to roar.*"

Risio sang:

"*Now goatishly to whore.*"

This society regarded goats as lusty animals.

Halfpenny sang:

"*Now hoggishly in the mire.*"

Lucio sang:

"*Now flinging hats in the fire.*"

All sang:

"*Iô, Bacchus! At thy table,*

"*Make us of thy reeling rabble.*"

They went inside the tavern.

— 2.2 —

Alone, Memphio said to himself: "I wonder that I hear no news about or from Dromio. Either he slacks the matter, or he betrays his master, I dare not broach anything to Stellio until I know what my serving-boy has done. I'll hunt him out; if the loitersack — idle boy — has gone springing into a tavern, I'll fetch him reeling out."

Dromio would be staggering from Memphio's blows, not from being drunk.

Memphio was the father of Accius, and Memphio wanted him to marry Silena.

Memphio went into the tavern.

Alone, Stellio entered the scene and said to himself:

"Without a doubt Risio has gone beyond himself and has overreached himself, in casting beyond the Moon."

"To cast beyond the Moon" means "to try to do more than one is capable of doing."

Stellio continued talking to himself:

"I fear the boy has run mad with studying and racking his brains, for I know he loved me so well, that for my favor he will venture to run out of his wits and risk going insane, and it may be, to quicken his invention and stimulate his brain, he has gone into this ivy-bush — this tavern — a notable nest for a grape owl."

"Grape owl" was slang for a person who stayed up late at night drinking.

Stellio continued talking to himself:

"I'll ferret him out, yet in the end I will treat him in a friendly manner. I cannot be merry until I hear what has been done in the marriages."

Stellio was the father of Silena, and he wanted her to marry Accius.

Stellio went into the tavern.

Alone, Prisius entered the scene and said to himself:

41

"I think Lucio has gone hunting squirrels, but I'll squirrel him — I'll hunt him and treat him like a squirrel — for it. I sent him on my errand, but I must go for an answer myself. I have tied up — confined — the loving worm my daughter, and I will see whether one fancy can worm another fancy out of her head.

"This green nosegay — the ivy bush, aka the tavern — I fear that my serving-boy has sniffed, for if he gets just a penny in his purse, he turns it suddenly into *argentum potabile*, I must search every place for him, for I stand on thorns — I am anxious — until I hear what he has done."

Argentum potabile is "drinkable silver," aka drinkable alcohol beverages that have been bought with a silver coin.

Prisius was the father of Livia, and he wanted her to marry Accius. Livia, however, wanted to marry Candius.

He exited into the tavern.

Alone, Sperantus entered the scene and said to himself:

"Well, be as be may is no banning."

In other words: As things stand now, there is no wedding banns. A wedding banns is a public announcement in a church of an upcoming marriage between a man and a woman who are engaged to each other.

Sperantus continued talking to himself:

I think I have charmed my young master: my son. A hungry meal, a ragged coat, and a dry cudgel — little food, ragged clothing, and a beating — have put him quite beside his love and his logic, too. He no longer thinks of love and learning. Besides, his pigsney — Livia — is put up, aka confined, and therefore now I'll let him take the air, and follow — pursue — Stellio's daughter, Silena, with all his learning, if he means to be my heir."

A "pigsney" is literally a pig's eye; it is used figuratively as a term of endearment.

"The boy has wit *sans* — without — measure. He has more than he needs. He has scraps of intelligence left over to serve as cat food and dog food, such is his advantage when it comes to intelligence.

"Well, without Halfpenny all my wit is not worth a dodkin — a small Dutch coin. That mite is miching — that small fellow is playing truant — in this grove — this tavern — for as long as his name is Halfpenny, he will be banqueting for the other halfpenny."

Halfpenny may be eating so that he can grow twice as big as he is now and so that he will then be called a full penny rather than a halfpenny.

Sperantus was the father of Candius, and he wanted him to marry Silena. Candius, however, wanted to marry Livia.

Sperantus exited into the tavern.

— 2.3 —

Alone, Candius said to himself:

"He must necessarily go whom the devil drives. My devil is a father, a fiend, who seeks to place affection by appointment, and to force love by compulsion. He seeks to make me love whomever he chooses. I have sworn to woo Silena, but it shall be so coldly that she shall take as small delight in my words, as I do contentment in his commandment. I'll teach him one school trick in love. But look! Who is that who comes out of Stellio's house? It seems to be Silena by her attire."

Candius still loved and wanted to marry Livia, but he had promised to woo Silena. His plan was to woo Silena so badly that she would not want to marry him.

Silena entered the scene.

Candius continued talking to himself:

"By her face I am sure it is she. Oh, fair face! Oh, lovely countenance! How are you now, Candius? If thou begin to slip at beauty suddenly, thou will surfeit with carousing — drinking — it at the last. Remember that Livia is faithful, aye, and let thine eyes witness that Silena is amiable."

He was taken by Silena's beauty, so taken that he thought he could love her.

Candius continued talking to himself:

"Here I shall please my father and myself. I will learn to be obedient, and come what will, I'll make a way.

"If she seems coy, I'll practice all the art of love; if I find her to be wise and cunning, I'll practice all the pleasures of love."

Silena really was beautiful — so beautiful that Candius was thinking of obeying his father's wishes.

Thinking that she was alone, Silena said to herself:

"My name is Silena. I don't care who knows it. I really don't.

"My father keeps me locked up, so he does, and now I have stolen out, so I have, to go to old Mother Bombie to know my fortune, so I will, for I have as fair a face as ever trod on shoe sole, and I have as free a foot as ever looked with two eyes."

Silena was beautiful, but she was not good with words, as her last sentence demonstrated: Faces don't tread on the ground, and feet don't look with two eyes.

Candius said to himself:

"What! I think she is either lunatic or foolish!"

He had heard her last sentence.

Candius continued speaking to himself:

"Thou are a fool, Candius.

"So fair a face cannot be the scabbard of a foolish mind, but she may be mad, for commonly in beauty that is so rare and splendid, there fall extreme passions."

He believed that she must be insane, not foolish. Beauty and foolishness do not go together. So said Candius.

Candius continued speaking to himself:

"Love and beauty disdain a mean, not therefore because beauty is no virtue, but because it is happiness, and we scholars know that virtue is not to be praised, but it is to be honored."

Aristotle believed that virtue is a mean between extremes. For example, courage is the mean between the extremes of foolhardiness (too much courage) and cowardice (too little courage). Happiness, however, is good in itself, and it is the chief good of human life, and the mean between extremes does not apply to it.

Candius continued speaking to himself:

"I will put on my best grace."

He stepped forward and said to Silena:

"Sweet wench, thy face is lovely, thy body is comely, and all that the eyes can see is enchanting. You see how — despite being unacquainted to you — I am bold to board you."

By "board," Candius meant "court, aka woo."

The phrase "board you" can be bawdy: to board — to climb on top of — you and have sex with you.

In her reply, Silena used "board" to mean "feed," as in "room and board."

She replied, "My father boards me already; therefore, I don't care even if your name were Geoffrey."

The expression "Farewell, gentle Geoffrey" appears in the play *Mankind*, circa 1475. The speaker is the unthrifty guest Nought, who is speaking to Mercy, who is grateful to have Nought and two other unthrifty guests leave.

Candius said to himself:

"She raves or over-reaches."

If Silena were insane, she would rave. If Silena were foolish, she would over-reach her intelligence: try to be witty but fail.

Candius then said out loud to Silena:

"I am one sweet soul who loves you, brought hither by report of your beauty, and here I languish with your rareness and splendidness."

Silena said, "I thank you that you would call."

Candius was not wooing in such a way that would intentionally cause her to reject him.

"I will always call on such a saint, one who has power to release my sorrows," Candius said. "Yield, fair creature to love!"

"I am none of that sect," Silena said.

The Family of Love was a religious sect that believed in the service of love. It denied the doctrine of the Trinity and opposed infant baptism.

Or possibly, Silena was saying that she could not be seduced.

"The loving sect is an ancient sect and an honorable sect, and therefore should be in a person so perfect," Candius said.

Silena said, "Much!"

This use of "Much!" means "Bah!"

"I love thee much," Candius said. "Give me one word of comfort."

Silena said, "In faith, sir, no, and so tell your master."

"I have no master, but I have come to make choice of a mistress," Candius said.

Silena said, "Aha, are you there with your bears?"

A man heard a sermon he did not like about Eliza and the bears: 2 Kings 2:23-24. Therefore, the following Sunday he went to a different church, only to see the same preacher, who again spoke about Elisha and the bears.

Silena's question means: Are you talking about that same old topic again?

Baffled by Silena's question, Candius said to himself:

"Doubtless, she is an idiot of the newest cut — the newest fashion. I'll once more test her."

He said out loud:

"I have loved thee long, Silena."

This was a lie.

"In your tother — your other — hose!" Silena said.

Once again, she was saying, "Bah!"

Candius said to himself:

"She is too simple to be natural, and she is too senseless to be artificial."

A natural is a born fool. An artificial fool is an actor playing the part of a fool.

Candius was wondering what Silena was.

He then said out loud:

"You said you went to know your fortune. I am a scholar and am cunning in palmistry."

"The better for you sir, so here's my hand," Silena said. "What time is it?"

This is not the kind of question one asks a fortune-teller unless one is a fool — or a wit.

Groucho Marx once went to a fortune-teller who claimed to know the wisdom of the universe. He asked her, "What's the capital of South Dakota?"

Candius examined Silena's hand and said, "The line of life is good. Venus' mount is very perfect. You shall have a scholar as your first husband."

Candius was a scholar.

Venus' mount is 1) the fleshy base of the thumb, and 2) the mons Veneris of the female genitalia.

Silena said:

"You are well seen in crones' dirt and in cranes' dirt."

A crone is an ugly old woman. Such a woman could be a fortune-teller such as Candius was pretending to be. Candius was using his "fortune-telling" to push the idea that Silena would marry him and be his bedfellow. Silena had seemingly shown no interest in him, and so such a suggestion was unethical and dirty.

A "crane" can be 1) a long-legged bird, and 2) a head.

Candius had dirt in his head. So said Silena.

Selena then said:

"Your father was a poulter."

A poulter is an official in charge of buying poultry. Such positions are in the royal court, a monastery, etc. If Selena is saying the Candius' father was a poulter in a monastery, she is calling him a bastard.

Silena laughed.

"Why do you laugh?" Candius asked.

"Because you should see my teeth," Silena said.

If he thought that he could tell her fortune by looking at her palm, why not have him look at her teeth? Both forms of fortune-telling make the same lack of sense.

Or perhaps she wouldn't mind biting him and causing him pain. After all, some people ought to be better strangers.

Candius said to himself:

"Alas, poor wench, I see now also thy folly. A fair fool is like a fresh weed with pleasing leaves and sour juice."

He had almost made up his mind that she was a fool.

He then said to himself:

"I will not yet leave her, for she may dissemble."

It was still possible that she was pretending that she was a fool.

If that were true, then she wanted to get rid of him by pretending to be a fool.

Candius said out loud to her:

"I cannot choose but love thee."

"I had thought to ask you," Silena said.

In this society, this was a mocking retort.

Candius said, "So then farewell, You are either too proud to accept me, or too simple and foolish to understand me."

He still was not certain that she was a fool.

"You need not be so crusty," Silena said. "You are not so hard baked."

She was punning and using a bakery metaphor. Puns and metaphors are signs of intelligence.

Candius said to himself:

"Now I perceive thy folly, who has raked together all the odd blind phrases that help them who do not know how to discourse, but when they cannot answer wisely, either with gibing and joking they cover their rudeness, or by some new-coined byword, they reveal their peevishness."

The word "rude" can mean 1) impolite, 2) uneducated, 3) unsophisticated, and/or 4) common.

Candius continued saying to himself:

"I am glad of this. Now I shall have color — a reason — to refuse the marriage match, and my father shall have reason to accept Livia as his daughter-in-law. I will go home, and I will repeat to my father the 'wise' encounter of me and her, and he shall perceive that there is nothing as fulsome and nauseating as a she-fool."

He exited.

Candius had made up his mind that Silena was a fool.

One reason for thinking that was that she used many proverbial sentences. Candius believed that Silena was a fool who let clichés do her thinking for her.

But if Silena's purpose had been to drive him away, she had succeeded.

If.

Alone, Silena said to herself:

"Good God, I think gentlemen had never less wit in a year. We maidens are mad wenches. We gird them and flout them and taunt them out of all scotch and notch — that is, completely — and they cannot see it."

According to Silena, she had not meant to drive him away. She was simply teasing him, the way that pretty young women do, and he did not like being teased.

Lack of communication had occurred between Candius and Silena. Lack of communication is common between men and women.

David Bruce once went on a first date with a woman who, at the end of the date, welcomed him into her circle of friends. He thought he had been friend-zoned, but he liked talking to the woman and asked if they could continue to watch movies and eat Chinese food together. She was agreeable, and for four months they did that without any hugging, kissing, holding hands, and so on. She then ghosted him. Later, he learned that she had ghosted him because he "didn't act like a boyfriend." His reaction was this:

"Boyfriend? I was a boyfriend? I wish I had known."

Silena continued talking to herself:

"I will learn from the old woman — Mother Bombie — whether I am a maiden or not, and then if I am not, I must necessarily be a man."

A maiden is 1) a virgin, and 2) a young unmarried woman.

Silena did not distinguish between the two meanings. She had no sexual experience yet, and she was not married, and so both meanings applied to her. She did not need to ask Mother Bombie if she — Silena — is a virgin.

But this society had a double standard. Unmarried women were supposed to be virgins. Unmarried men were expected not to be virgins. In this society, if Silena were not a virgin, then she needed to be a man.

Silena wanted to ask Mother Bombie not about her — Silena's — present life, but instead about her — Silena's — future life. Would Silena remain an unmarried virgin, or would she be married?

Silena called out a blessing:

"May God be here."

Mother Bombie opened the door of her home.

She asked, "Who's there?"

"One who would be a maiden," Silena said.

After meeting with and speaking to Candius, she wanted to remain unmarried.

"If thou are not a maiden, it is impossible thou should be, and it is a shame thou are not," Mother Bombie said.

"They say you are a witch," Silena said.

"They lie," Mother Bombie said. "I am a cunning woman. I am a wise woman."

"Then tell me something," Silena said.

Mother Bombie told her something:

"Hold up thy hand — not so high."

In other words: Don't be so proud.

Also, Mother Bombie was looking at Silena's palm.

Mother Bombie continued:

"Thy 'father' knows thee not."

In other words: Your "father" does not know you. Of course, Silena could not hear the quotation marks around the word "father."

Mother Bombie continued:

"Thy 'mother' bare thee not."

In other words: Your "mother" did not give birth to you.

"Falsely bred, truly begot."

In other words: You were falsely raised (brought up by the wrong parents), but you were truly begotten.

"Truly" can mean "legitimately." Silena's parents were married.

Mother Bombie continued:

"Choice of two husbands, but never tied in banns."

In other words: You have the choice of two men to be your husband, but you are not now married.

The two men who could marry Silena are Accius and Candius.

Mother Bombie continued:

"Because of love and natural bonds."

In other words: Because of love and the bonds of kinship.

Like the words of many fortune-tellers, interpretation can be difficult, or if the words seem clear, they can also seem unbelievable.

Silena rejected the fortune-teller's words.

Imitating the rhythm of Mother Bombie's words, Silena said:

"I thank you for nothing,

"Because I understand nothing."

Fools tend to think that they know things that they do not know.

Wise people such as Socrates know when they don't know something.

Silena continued:

"Although you are as old as you are,

"Yet I am as young as I am,

"And because I am so fair,

"Therefore, you are so foul."

In other words: You are jealous of my youth and beauty, and therefore you told me a foul fortune.

Selina continued:

"And so farewell, frost,

"My fortune naught me cost."

The telling of her fortune would cost her nothing because she would not pay.

Silena exited.

Alone, Mother Bombie said to herself:

"Farewell, fair fool.

"Little do thou know thy hard fortune, but in the end thou shall, and that must reveal what no one can discover.

"In the meantime, I will profess cunning for all who come here."

Mother Bombie closed the door to her house.

— 2.4 —

Dromio, Risio, Halfpenny, and Lucio met together.

All of them were serving-boys plotting against their masters.

Their masters had recently found them drinking in the tavern, but the serving-boys had slipped away, leaving the bill behind for their masters to pay.

Dromio said, "We were all taken tardy — that is, taken unawares. We were not expecting our masters."

"Our masters will be overtaken if they tarry," Risio said.

The masters were in the tavern: They would be overcome by alcohol if they tarried and drank in the tavern.

"Now everyone must make an excuse by using their wit, and every excuse must be trickery," Halfpenny said.

"Let us remember our complot — that is, our joint plan," Lucio said.

Dromio said:

"We will all plod — work — on that.

"Oh, the wine has turned my wit to vinegar!"

"You mean it is sharp," Risio said.

"Sharp?" Halfpenny said. "I'll guarantee that it will serve for as good sauce to knavery as —"

"As what? Lucio said.

"As thy knavery serves as meat — food — for Dromio's wit," Halfpenny said.

"We must all give a reckoning for our day's travail," Dromio said.

They had to give an account of what they had done that day — and pay the consequences.

Risio said:

"Huh, I am glad we escaped the reckoning — the bill — for our liquor.

"If you are examined about how we met, swear that we met by chance, for so they met, and therefore they will believe it.

"If you are examined about how much we drank, let them answer the question themselves: They know best because they paid it."

"We must not tarry," Halfpenny said. "*Abeundum est mihi*: I must remove myself. I must go and cast this matter in a corner."

The word "cast" means "vomit."

He was going to be sick.

Dromio said:

"Aye, *prae, sequar*. You go ahead, and I'll follow. Get a bowl to be sick in, and I'll come after you with a broom to clean up any mess.

"Let everyone remember his own cue."

All of them needed to remember his own part in the plan.

Risio said, "Aye, and everyone remember his key, or else we shall thrive ill."

All of them needed to remember when they could speak freely and when they needed to keep their lips locked.

"When shall we meet?" Halfpenny asked.

"Tomorrow fresh and fasting," Risio said.

By "fasting," he meant "before breakfast."

"Fast eating our meat, for we have drunk for tomorrow, and tomorrow we must eat for today," Dromio said.

Today, they had drunk enough for two days, but they had not eaten. As far as food was concerned, they were fasting.

Tomorrow, they would not drink, but they would eat fast and break their fast because they had to eat enough for two days: today and tomorrow.

"Away, away. Let's leave, for if our masters take us here, the matter is marred," Halfpenny said.

"Let everyone go to his task," Lucio said.

They exited.

— 2.5 —

Memphio, Stellio, Prisius, and Sperantus spoke together. They were tipsy from being in the tavern.

They were all fathers of marriageable children.

Memphio said, "How luckily we met suddenly in a tavern, we who have not drunk together almost these thirty years."

Stellio said:

"A tavern is the rendezvous, the exchange, the staple for good fellows."

A tavern was a place where businessmen met to exchange news while drinking.

A staple is a place where trade is conducted.

Stellio continued:

"I have heard my great-grandfather tell how his great-grandfather would say that it was an old proverb when his great-grandfather was a child that it was a good wind that blew a man to the wine."

Prisius said:

"The old time was a good time.

"Ale was an ancient drink, and our ancestors considered it authentical and with high regard.

"Gascony wine was liquor for a lord, sack a medicine for the sick, and I may tell you, he who had a cup of red wine to go with his oysters was in the Queen's subsidy book."

People in the Queen's subsidy book were wealthy enough to provide extra money to Queen Elizabeth I when required.

Sperantus said:

"Aye, but now you see how loose this age has grown.

"Our serving-boys carouse sack like double — like strong — beer, and they say that which does an old man good, can do a young man no harm.

"Our serving-boys say that old men eat pap, aka baby food, so why shouldn't children drink sack. Our serving-boys say that the old men's white heads have time out of mind cheated our serving-boys' young years."

Memphio said:

"Well, the world has become wanton since I knew it first.

"Our serving-boys put as much now in their bellies in an hour as would clothe their whole bodies in a year. We have paid eight shillings for their tippling, and as I have heard, eight shillings was as much as bought Rufus, sometime king of this land, a pair of hose."

Rufus is King William II (reigned 1087-1100). Because of his red hair, he was called William Rufus. An anecdote about him states that he rejected a pair of hose because they were too inexpensive for a king to wear, but he accepted a second pair of hose that were inferior to the first pair after being told that the second pair of hose cost more than the first pair of hose.

"Is it possible?" Prisius asked.

Stellio said:

"Oh, it is true.

"The serving-boys say that ale is out of request — it is out of fashion. They said that ale is hogs' porridge, broth for beggars, a caudle for constables, watchmen's mouth-glue. The better the ale is, the more like bird lime it is, and they say that ale never makes one staid and stayed — sober and still — except in the stocks."

The serving-boys had been drinking wine rather than ale, which was usually drunk by the lower social classes.

Hogs' porridge is pig slop.

A caudle is a medicinal drink.

Ale is watchmen's mouth-glue: A bribe of some drinks can keep a watchman's mouth shut.

Bird lime is a sticky substance used to catch birds.

One reason for people at this time to drink so much was that alcohol killed bad germs in the liquor. Ale and wine were safe to drink.

"I'll teach my wag-halter to know grapes from barley," Memphio said.

A "wag" is a high-spirited boy who is very capable of causing trouble.

A wag-halter is a noose for a wag such as any of the serving-boys.

Ale was made from barley, and wine was made from grapes, which were more expensive than barley. Memphio was going to teach his gallows-bird, Dromio, to drink ale, not wine.

"And I will teach mine to discern a spigot from a faucet," Prisius said.

Wine was dispensed from a spigot, and ale was dispensed from a faucet.

"And I will teach mine to judge the difference between a black bowl and a silver goblet," Sperantus said.

"And my serving-boy shall learn the odds — the difference — between a stand and a hogshead, yet I cannot choose but laugh to see how my wag answered me, when I struck him for drinking sack," Sperantus said.

A stand is a barrel for beer or ale.

A hogshead is a large barrel that can hold wine.

A wag is a mischievous boy.

Sack is white wine.

"Why, what did he say?" Prisius asked.

Stellio said:

"He told me:

"'Master, sack is the most sovereign and most supreme drink in the world, and the safest for all times and weathers.

"'If it thunders, though all the ale and beer in the town turn and go sour, wine will be constant and retain its freshness.

"'If lighting flashed, and if any fire comes to it, it is the most apt wine to burn and the most wholesome when it is burnt.

"'So much for Summer.'"

Burnt sack is heated sack, or it is wine sweetened with burned sugar.

Stellio continued:

"'If it freezes, why, then sack is so hot in operation that no ice can congeal it.

"'If it rains, why, then he who cannot abide the heat of sack, may put in — add — water.

"'So much for Winter.'

"And so ran his way of speaking, and so he ran off, but I'll overtake him."

Stellio would catch his serving-boy, Risio.

Sperantus said, "Who would think that my hop-on-my-thumb, Halfpenny, scarcely as high as a pint pot, would reason and argue the matter; but he learned his leer of — his lesson from — my son, Candius, his young master, whom I have brought up at Oxford, and whom I think must continue his learning here in Kent at Ashford."

His education would be learning how to farm.

"Why, what did Halfpenny say to you?" Memphio asked.

Sperantus said, "He boldly rapped it out: *Sine Ceres and Bacchus friget Venus*. He rapped out that without wine and sugar, his veins would wax — grow — cold."

The Latin means: Without Ceres and Bacchus, Venus grows cold.

Ceres is the goddess of agriculture, and Bacchus is the god of wine and ecstasy, so metaphorically "Ceres and Bacchus" means "bread and wine."

Memphio said out loud:

"The serving-boys were all in a pleasant and jocular vein, but I must be gone, and I must get an account of my serving-boy's business, and so farewell, neighbors. God knows when we shall meet again."

Memphio then said to himself:

"Yet I have revealed nothing; my wine has been my wit's friend.

"I long to hear what Dromio has done."

The four serving-boys were working together, but the four masters were keeping secret plots from each other.

Memphio exited.

Stellio said out loud:

"I cannot stay, but this good fellowship shall cost me the setting on at our next meeting."

He would pay the bill of their next meeting.

Stellio then said to himself:

"I am glad I blabbed nothing about the marriage, now I hope to compass it and bring it about. I know my serving-boy has been bungling about it."

Stellio exited.

Prisius said out loud:

"Let us all go, for I must go to my clothes that hang on the tenters to dry."

Prisius then said to himself:

"My boy shall hang with them, if he does not give me a satisfactory account of his day's work."

Prisius exited.

Alone, Sperantus said to himself:

"If all are gone, I'll not stay.

"I am sure that Halfpenny has done me a penny's worth of good, else I'll spend his body in buying a rod to beat him with."

Sperantus exited.

CHAPTER 3
— 3.1 —

Maestius and Serena talked together. They were brother and sister; they were the children of Vicinia, a nurse.

As a wet-nurse, Vicinia had breast-fed the infants of wealthy people.

Maestius said, "Sweet sister, I don't know how it comes to pass, but I find in myself passions more than brotherly."

Serena said, "And I, dear brother, find my thoughts entangled with affections beyond nature, which so flame into my distempered, disordered head that I can neither without danger smother the fire, nor without modesty — without shame — disclose my fury."

Although they were brother and sister, they were attracted to each other in a way not condoned by society.

"Our parents are poor, our love is unnatural, what can then happen to make us happy and fortunate?" Maestius asked.

"Only to be content with our father's mean estate, to combat against our own intemperate desires, and to yield to the success — that is, the outcome — of fortune, who although she has framed — that is, has made — us miserable, cannot make us monstrous," Serena said.

They might be sexually attracted to each other, but that did not mean that they had to give in to their passions.

Maestius said, "It is good counsel, fair sister, if the necessity of love could be relieved by counsel, yet this is our comfort: These unnatural heats have stretched and extended themselves no further than thoughts, although I am unhappy that they should stretch and reach so far."

In fact, they had not given in to their sexual desire for each other.

Serena said, "Strange it seems in sense: That which nature warrants, laws forbid. Because thou are mine, therefore thou must not be mine."

Brother and sister ought to love each other, but because Maestius was her brother, he must not be her husband.

Maestius said, "So it is, Serena, the nearer we are in blood, the further we must be from love, and the greater the kindred is, the less the kindness and affection must be, so that between brothers and sisters superstition — irrational belief — has made affection and love cold, but between strangers custom has bred love exquisite."

Maestius seemed tempted to engage in incest, since he believed that the prohibitions against it were based in superstition.

"They say there is nearby an old cunning woman who can tell fortunes, expound dreams, tell about things that are lost, and divine — prophesy — accidents and incidents to come," Serena said. "She is called the good woman, who yet never did any hurt."

"Nor did she do any good, I think, Serena," Maestius said, "yet to satisfy thy mind we will see what she can say."

"Good brother, let us," Serena said.

"Who is within?" Maestius asked loudly in front of Mother Bombie's door.

Mother Bombie opened the door.

She said, "The dame of the house."

"She might have said the beldam because of her face, and her years, and her attire — her looks, her old age, and her clothing," Maestius said.

A "beldame" is a hag or witch.

Serena said, "Good mother, tell us, if by your cunning you can, what shall become of my brother and me."

Mother Bombie said:

"Let me see your hands, and look at me steadfastly with your eyes."

She looked at their hands and their faces, and then she foretold their future:

"You shall be married tomorrow hand in hand,

"By the laws of good nature and the land.

"Your parents shall be glad and give you their land.

"You shall each of you displace a fool,

"And both of you together must relieve a fool."

The marriage she foretold would be in accordance with "the laws of good nature and the land"; that is, it would be a completely valid marriage that violated no laws of church or society.

She then said:

"If this is not true, then call me an old fool."

Imitating her, Maestius said:

"This is my sister, and so we cannot marry.

"Our parents are poor and have no land to give us.

"Each of us is a fool

"To come for counsel to such an old fool."

Serena said:

"These doggerel rhymes and obscure words, coming out of the mouth of such a weather-beaten witch, are thought to be divinations of some holy spirit, but they are only the dreams of decayed brains.

"For my own part, I wish that thou might sit on that stool" — she pointed to a stool — "until he and I marry by law."

Mother Bombie said, "I say that Mother Bombie never speaks but once, and yet never spoke untruth once."

"Come, brother, let us go to our poor home," Serena said. "This — to reveal our passions — is our comfort, since we cannot enjoy our love."

Maestius said, "Be content, sweet sister, and learn from me hereafter that these old saws — old sayings — of such old hags are only false fires to lead one out of a plain path into a deep pit."

Witches and cunning women can be deceptive and try to lead their hearers into losing their souls. Think of the witches in *Macbeth*.

Mother Bombie, however, had the reputation of being a good woman.

Maestius and Serena exited, and Mother Bombie shut her door.

— 3.2 —

Dromio and Risio entered the scene from different directions.

They were serving-boys plotting against their masters.

Dromio's master was Memphio, and Risio's master was Stellio.

Not seeing Risio, Dromio said to himself, "*Ingenium quondam fuerat pretiosius auro*: The time was wherein wit would work like wax and crock up gold like honey."

The Latin means: At one time, genius — wit and intelligence — was more precious than gold.

Something that works like wax (which is pliable) is easily accomplished.

Gold and honey were both stored in earthenware vessels.

Noticing Dromio, Risio said, "*At nunc barbarie est grandis habere nihil*: But now wit and honesty buy nothing in the market."

The Latin means: But now it is the greatest barbarism to have nothing.

Seeing Risio, Dromio said, "What! Risio! How are thou doing after thy potting?"

"Potting" means drinking out of pots: drinking vessels.

Risio said:

"My master, Stellio, wrung all in the tavern, and he thrust all out in the house."

Stellio had gotten rid of all Risio's wine by wringing and thrusting.

First, he had stopped the drinking by showing up at the tavern. "Wrung all in the tavern" can mean "caused everyone distress in the tavern."

In addition, he could have metaphorically wrung all the wine out of a cloth that soaked up spilled wine. He would literally have stopped the flow of wine.

Second, he had caused Risio to vomit the wine later in the master's house. The word "thrust" can mean "expel." It can also mean "squeeze." Stellio may have squeezed Risio's stomach to make him vomit.

Risio then asked:

"But how are thou doing?"

Dromio said:

"I? It would be a day's work to tell thee about it.

"My master, Memphio, spoke nothing but sentences, but they were vengeable — they were terribly — long ones, for when one word was out, he made a pause of a quarter of an hour long until he spoke another.

"Sentences" are moral maxims.

"Why, what did he do in all that time?" Risio asked.

Dromio said, "He broke interjections as if they were wind: *eho*, *ho*, *oi*."

"Wind" is flatulence.

Eho is Latin for "woe!" It also means "hey!"

Ho is Latin for "ho!"

Oi is Latin for "oh!"

"And what did thou do?" Risio asked.

"Answer him in his own language, as *evax*, *vah*, *hui*," Dromio said.

Possibly, Dromio farted.

Evax is Latin for "yes!" It also means "hurray" and "escape."

Vah is Latin for "woe!" and "alas!" It also means "wow!"

Hui is Latin for "ah!" It also means "here."

Risio said:

"These were conjunctions rather than interjections.

Dromio's words said in response to Memphio had more than one meaning. They meant one thing *and* another thing.

"But what about the plot?"

Dromio said, "As we agreed, I told Memphio that I understood that Silena was very wise, and she could sing exceedingly well, and I told him that my plan was, seeing that Accius, his son, was a proper and handsome youth, and could also sing sweetly, that he should come in the nick of time — the right time — when she was singing and answer her."

Accius and Silena would meet by singing a song together outside.

"Excellent," Risio said.

Dromio then said:

"Then he asked how it should be devised that she might come abroad — that is, come outside. I told him that was taken account of already by my plan.

"After the song will have ended, and after they will have seen one another, noting the apparel, and marking each other's personal appearances, he — Memphio — will call in his son, Accius, for fear he should over-reach his speech and betray himself as a simpleton by saying too much."

"Very good," Risio said.

Dromio continued:

"Then I said to Memphio that I had gotten a young gentleman who resembled his son in years and favor — in age and appearance. This young man, while wearing Accius' apparel, would court Silena. She would find the young man wise, and after that, by small entreaty she would be won without more words, and so the marriage would be agreed to and arranged by this cozenage and trickery, and his son would never speak a word for himself."

Risio said:

"Thou boy!

"I have done as agreed to in every point, for the song, the calling her in, and the hoping that another woman (wiser than Silena) shall woo Accius, and his daughter, Silena, shall wed Accius.

"I told my master, Stellio, the father of Silena, that this wooing would occur tonight, and they would be early married in the morning, without any words except those they will say after the priest."

Accius and Silena would speak no words to each other except the words of the wedding vows until after the wedding had been performed.

Dromio said:

"All this fodges — works out — well.

"Now if Halfpenny and Lucio have played their parts, we shall have excellent entertainment, and here they come."

Halfpenny and Lucio entered the scene.

They were also serving-boys plotting against their masters.

Dromio asked them:

"How wrought the wine, my lads?"

Halfpenny said, "How? Like wine, for my body being the rundlet, and my mouth the vent, it wrought — fermented — two days over, until I had thought the hoops of my head would have flown asunder."

A "rundlet" is a small cask or barrel.

Halfpenny was saying that his body was like a small barrel, and the wine was coming out of his mouth (in vomiting) like wine coming from a spigot so ferociously that he thought the hoops of the barrel — that is, the "hoops" of his head — would break.

Fermenting wine creates gas that can break the container in which it is confined.

In other words: Risio had a bad hangover.

Lucio said, "The best thing was that our masters were as well whittled — well drunk — as we, for yet they lie by it."

Their masters were still in bed with their hangovers.

Risio said, "All the better for us. We only parboiled — half-cooked — a little our livers, but our masters have sod — steeped and drowned — their livers in sack these past forty years."

Halfpenny said:

"That makes them spit white broth as they do."

"White broth" is spittle associated with drinking.

Halfpenny continued:

"But let's get to the purpose of our meeting.

"Candius and Livia will send their attires; you must send the apparel of Accius and Silena.

"Candius and Livia wonder why, but they commit the matter to our quadripartite — four-part — wit.

"If you keep your promise to get them married by your plan, and with their parents' consent, you shall have ten pounds apiece for your pains," Lucio said.

Dromio said:

"If we don't keep our promise, we are undone and ruined, for we have broached a cozenage — a trick — already, and my master, Memphio, has the tap in his hand, so that it must necessarily run out."

Dromio was using the metaphor of tapping a barrel of wine.

In other words: ... for we have started a deception already, and my master, Memphio, has already set it in motion, and it will run its course.

Dromio continued:

"Let Candius and Livia be ruled by us — follow our advice — and bring hither their apparel, and we will determine the outcome.

"The rest commit to our intricate considerations: All of us do what we have planned to do.

"Depart."

Halfpenny and Lucio exited.

Accius walked onto the scene.

Dromio said, "Here comes Accius tuning his pipes: warming up his singing voice. I perceive my master keeps touch — my master, Memphio, is keeping his agreement."

Silena walked onto the scene.

Risio said:

"And here comes Silena with her wit of proof: impenetrable wit.

"By the Virgin Mary, her wit will scarcely hold out question shot: It will scarcely hold up under a barrage of slight, easy-to-answer questions."

"Shot "consists of small pellets.

Risio added:

"Let us go in to instruct our masters in the cue."

They would tell their masters, Memphio and Stellio, what to do and when to do it: Memphio and Stellio would come outside and separate their children, Accius and Silena, after they had sung together.

Dromio said:

"Come, let's be jogging — let's be going.

"But wouldn't it be worth a world to hear them woo one another?"

"That shall be hereafter to make us sport and entertainment, but our masters shall never know it," Risio said.

Dromio and Risio exited into the houses of their masters.

Accius and Silena remained behind.

They sang together — well.

Accius sang:

"*O Cupid! Monarch over kings,*

"*Wherefore [Why] have thou feet and wings?*

"*It is to show how swift thou art,*

"*When thou wound a tender heart,*

"*Thy wings being clipped, and feet held still,*"

In other words: If thy wings were clipped, and thy feet were held still.

Accius continued to sing:

"*Thy bow so many could not kill.*"

When Cupid, god of love, shot someone with a golden arrow, that person fell in love.

Silena sang:

"*It is all one [It does not matter] in Venus' wanton school,*

"*Who highest sits, the wise man or the fool:*"

Venus is the sexually active goddess of sexual passion.

In Elizabethan schools, students were seated according to their academic ability. The most academically adept student was seated highest.

Silena continued to sing:

"*Fools in love's college*

"*Have far more knowledge,*

"*To read a woman over,*"

In other words: To understand a woman.

Silena continued to sing:

"*Than a neat, prating [a trim, prattling] lover.*"

Accius and Silena sang together:

"*Nay, it is confessed [everyone admits],*

"*That fools please women best.*"

Memphio and Stellio entered the scene.

Memphio said to his son, "Accius, go inside and that quickly. What! Walking outside without my permission?"

Stellio said to his daughter, "Silena, I ask you to look homeward. It is a cold air, and you don't have your muffler. Go home."

Accius and Silena exited inside their father's houses.

Memphio said to himself, "This is pat: All is going according to plan. If the rest of our plan proceeds well, Stellio is likely to marry his daughter to a fool — my son — but a bargain is a bargain."

Stellio said to himself:

"This frames to my wish: This is what I wanted to have happen.

"Memphio is likely to marry a fool — my daughter — to his son. Accius' tongue shall tie all Memphio's land to Silena's dowry; let his father's teeth undo them if he can."

A proverb stated, "He has tied a knot with his tongue that all his teeth cannot untie."

Stellio continued saying to himself:

"But here I see Memphio. I must seem kind and friendly, for in kindness lies cozenage — lies a cheat."

Memphio said to himself:

"Well, here is Stellio.

"I'll talk of other matters, and fly from the mark I shoot at, lapwing-like flying far from the place where I nestle."

Memphio would not talk about the wedding that he hoped would occur. He would be like a lapwing and draw Stellio's attention away from the wedding.

Lapwings were birds with nests on the ground. When a predator drew near the lapwing's nest, the lapwing would pretend to have a wounded wing and draw the predator away from the nest. When the predator was far enough away from the nest, the lapwing would take flight.

Memphio said out loud to Stellio, "What are you doing outside? I heard that you were sick since our last drinking bout."

Stellio said, "You see that gossipy reports are not truths, I heard the same thing about you, and we are both well. I perceive that sober men tell most lies, for in *vino veritas* — in wine there is truth. If they had drunk wine, they would have told the truth."

Memphio said, "Our serving-boys will be sure then never to lie, for they are always swilling wine, but Stellio, I must strain courtesy and be less than mannerly with you. I have business I cannot delay."

Stellio replied:

"That happens at a good time, Memphio, for I was about to ask for your patience to allow me to depart. I have business it is necessary for me to do."

He then said to himself:

"Perhaps I will move his patience and make him angry before long."

Memphio said to himself, "Good, silly — foolish — Stellio. We must buckle — argue — soon."

They exited.

— 3.3 —

Halfpenny, Lucio, and Rixula talked together.

Rixula was a serving-girl to Prisius.

Rixula was holding Livia's clothing, and Halfpenny was holding Candius' clothing.

Lucio said, "Come, Rixula, we have made thee privy to the whole pack; there lay down the pack."

The first "pack" meant "plot," and the second "pack" meant "bundle."

"I believe unless it is better handled, we shall be unemployed and out of doors," Rixula said.

Halfpenny said, "I don't care. *Omnem solum forti patria*. I can live in Christendom as well as in Kent."

The Latin means: To the brave, every land is his own country.

"And I'll sing *Patria ubicumque bene*. Every house is my home where I may stanch hunger," Lucio said.

The Latin meant: Wherever you do well is your country.

Rixula said, "If you set all on hazard and risk everything, although I am a poor wench, I am as hardy and brave as both of you. I cannot speak Latin, but I say in plain English that if anything falls out cross and badly for us, I'll run away."

"He loves thee well who would run after and pursue thee," Halfpenny said.

"Why, Halfpenny, there's no goose so gray in the lake that cannot find a gander for her mate," Rixula said.

In other words: Every woman, even if she is not conventionally attractive, can find a mate.

"I love a nut-brown lass," Lucio said. "It is good to recreate."

A nut-brown lass is a woman with a dark complexion.

Some kinds of recreation result in procreation.

"Thou mean: A brown nut is good to crack," Halfpenny said.

In other words: It is good to crack a brown nut open, and it is good for a dark-complexioned woman to open her legs.

"Why, wouldn't it do thee good to crack such a nut?" Lucio asked.

"I fear she is worm-eaten within — she is so moth-eaten without," Halfpenny said.

Rixula said, "If you take your pleasure of me, I'll go in and tell your masters your plots against them."

By "take your pleasure of me," Rixula meant "insult and mock me."

"Indeed, sour heart," Halfpenny said, "he who takes his pleasure on thee is very pleasurable."

By "takes your pleasure on thee," Halfpenny meant "has sex with you."

"Pleasurable" means "devoted to seeking pleasure."

Rixula said, "You mean knavishly, and yet I hope foul water will quench hot fire as soon as fair."

In other words: An ugly woman can satisfy sexual desire as well as a beautiful woman.

Halfpenny said, "Well, then, let fair words cool that choler and anger that foul speeches have kindled, and because we are all in this case, and we all hope to have good fortune, sing a roundelay, and we'll help. Sing a roundelay such as thou were accustomed to sing when thou beat hemp."

People convicted of small offenses were put to work beating hemp that would be used to make rope.

In Elizabethan slang, "beating hemp" meant "having sex."

Lucio said, "It was crabs she stamped, and she stole away one to make a crabby face for herself."

Rixula said, "I agree in hope that the hemp shall come to your wearing. A halfpenny halter may hang you both, that is, Halfpenny and you may hang in a halter."

A halter is a noose made of rope.

"Well brought about," Halfpenny said.

This meant 1) a good answer, and 2) a good conclusion.

"The halter will bring a good conclusion when it is about your neck," Rixula said.

"Now she's in, she will never out," Lucio said.

In other words: Now that she's started [insulting us], she'll never stop.

Rixula said:

"Nor when your heads are in the noose, as is likely to happen, they should not come out.

"But listen to my song:

Rixula sang:

"*Full hard I did sweat,*

"*When hemp I did beat.*

"*Then thought I of nothing but hanging,*

"*The hemp being spun,*

"*My beating was done,*"

After engaging in sexual intercourse, the penis hangs down.

Spinning consists of making threads. Sex can make threads of semen.

Rixula continued to sing:

"*Then I wished for a noise*"

A "noise" is a band of musicians.

"Noise" is also unwanted sound.

Rixula continued to sing:

"*Of crack-halter boys,*"

"Crack-halter boys" are boys who are destined to hang.

Necks crack when they are broken.

Rixula continued to sing:

"*On those hempen strings to be twanging.*"

One meaning of "to twang" is "to pluck," as in plucking the strings of a musical instrument.

Another meaning of "to twang" is "to twitch," as in twitching at the end of a rope while being hanged.

Rixula continued to sing:

"*Long looked I about,*

"*The city throughout —*"

Halfpenny and Lucio sang:

"*— and found no such fiddling varlets.*"

"Fiddling" can refer to engaging in sexual intercourse as well as to playing a fiddle.

Rixula sang:

"*Yes, at last coming hither,*

"*I saw four together.*"

Halfpenny and Lucio sang:

"*May thy hemp choke such singing harlots.*"

"Singing harlots" can mean noisy whores.

Rixula sang:

"'*Tu-whit tu-whoo,*' *the Owl does cry,*

"'*Phip, phip,*' *the Sparrows as they fly,*

"*The goose does hiss, the duck cries quack.*

"'*A rope,*' *the Parrot, that holds tack.*"

The owl is a night bird, and the night is associated with prostitutes.

This society considered sparrows lusty.

In this society, "goose" and "duck" were slang words for a prostitute.

In this society, parrots were often taught to say the word "rope."

The word "rope" can mean "penis" and "hanging penis" as well as a hanging noose.

The word "tack" means "to sail through the wind." If you are in a sailboat and the wind is blowing on the right side of your face and you tack through the wind, soon the wind will be blowing on the left side of your face. The place the wind hits your face changes, and the meaning of the word "rope" spoken by the parrot changes.

"Holds tack" may mean that the parrot repeats the one phrase it has been taught to speak.

Halfpenny and Lucio sang:

"*The parrot and the rope be thine.*"

Rixula sang:

"*The hanging yours, but the hemp mine.*"

Rixula will have the "hemp," the "rope," the penis: the sexual pleasure.

Dromio and Risio entered the scene from their masters' houses. Dromio was carrying Accius' clothing, and Risio was carrying Silena's clothing.

"Yonder stand the wags," Dromio said. "I have come in good time."

"All are here before me," Risio said. "You make haste."

Rixula said, "I believe you make haste to your hanging, for I think you have all robbed your masters. Here's every man his baggage."

Dromio and Risio were each holding a bundle of clothing.

Halfpenny said, "That is, we are all with thee, for thou are a very baggage."

The word "baggage" means strumpet.

Rixula said, "Hold thy peace, or on my honesty and chastity, I swear I'll buy a halfpenny purse with thee."

"Indeed, that's big enough to put thy honesty and chastity in, but come, shall we get on about the matter?" Dromio asked.

"Now that it has come to the pinch, my heart pants," Lucio said.

Halfpenny said, "I for my part am resolute. *In utrumque paratus*: ready to die or to run away."

The Latin means: I am prepared to go in either direction.

Lucio said, "But listen to me. I was troubled with a vile dream, and therefore it is little time spent to let Mother Bombie expound it; she is cunning in all things."

"Then I will know my fortune," Dromio said.

"And I'll ask about a silver spoon that was lost yesterday, which I must pay for," Rixula said.

"And I'll know what will happen with our plots," Risio said.

"And I'll learn that, too," Halfpenny said.

"Then let us all go quickly," Dromio said. "We must not sleep in this business; our masters are so watchful about it."

They went to Mother Bombie's house and knocked on her door.

Mother Bombie asked, "Why do you rap so hard at the door?"

"Because we would come in," Dromio said.

"My house is no inn," Mother Bombie said, opening the door.

"Cross yourselves," Halfpenny said. "Make the sign of the cross. Look how evil she looks."

"Don't look directly at her," Dromio said. "She'll turn us all into apes."

"What do you want with me?" Mother Bombie asked.

"They say that you are cunning, and they say that you are called the good woman of Rochester," Risio said.

The location was a street in Rochester, Kent, England.

"If never to do harm is to do good, I dare say I am not ill — not bad," Mother Bombie said. "But what's the matter?"

"I had an ill dream, and I desire to know the signification and meaning," Lucio said.

Mother Bombie said:

"Dreams, my son, have their weight. Although they are of a troubled mind, yet they are signs of fortune.

"Continue to speak."

Lucio said:

"In the dawning of the day, for about that time by my starting out of my sleep, I found it to be, I thought I saw a stately piece of beef, with a cape-cloak of cabbage, embroidered with pepper, having two honorable pages with hats of mustard on their heads, the beef himself in great pomp and state sitting upon a cushion of white brewish [broth-soaked bread], lined with brown bread."

This society considered early-morning dreams to be truthful.

The piece of beef is described as being a nobleman sitting in state.

A cape-cloak is a cloak with a short cape over the shoulders.

Lucio continued:

"I thought being powdered [with salt], he was much troubled with the salt rheum [runny nose], and therefore there stood by him two great flagons of sack and beer: the sack to dry up his rheum, and the beer to quench his choler and anger.

"I, as one envying his ambition [pride of state], hungering and thirsting after his honor, began to pull his cushion from under him, hoping by that means to give him a fall and bring him down, and with putting out my hand I awakened, and I found nothing in all this dream about me except the salt rheum."

Dromio said, "This is a dream for a butcher."

Lucio said:

"Quiet. Let me finish recounting my dream.

"Then I slumbered again, and I thought there came in a leg of mutton."

"What! All gross meat and large joints," Dromio said. "A rack would have been dainty."

A rack is a neck or ribs eaten in broth.

Lucio said, "Thou fool, how could it come in, unless it had been a leg? I thought his hose were cut and drawn out with parsley. I thrust my hand into my pocket for a knife, thinking to hox him, and so awakened."

A fashion of the time was to cut hose to allow the underlying material to show through.

The parsley was used to dress the joint.

"To hox him" means "to cut his hamstrings."

Mother Bombie said, "It is likely thou went supperless to bed."

Hunger is a reason to dream about food.

"So I do every night but Sundays," Lucio said. "Prisius, my master, has a weak stomach, and therefore we must starve."

Mother Bombie said, "Well, take this for thy answer, although the dream is fantastical.

"They who in the morning sleep dream of eating

"Are in danger of sickness, or of beating,

"Or shall hear of a wedding fresh a beating."

"Fresh a beating" means "in the making."

"This may be true," Lucio said.

Halfpenny said:

"Then let me come in with a dream, short but sweet, with the result that my mouth waters ever since I woke.

"I thought there sat upon a shelf three damask prunes [damsons] in velvet caps and pressed satin gowns like judges, and that there were a whole handful of currants to be arraigned of a riot, because they clung together in such clusters.

"Twelve raisins of the sun were empaneled in a jury, and as a leaf of whole mace, which was the bailiff, who was carrying the quest [leading away the jury at the inquest] to consult, I thought there came an angry cook, and gelded the jury of their stones, and swept both judges, jurors, rebels, and bailiff into a porridge pot, at which being melancholy, I fetched a deep sigh that woke myself and my bedfellow."

Sun-raisins are grapes that are dried on the vine by the sun.

"Mace" is a spice that is made from the outer covering of the nutmeg.

A mace is also a staff of office that a bailiff carries.

"Stones" are 1) grape pips, and 2) testicles.

Dromio said, "This was devised — made up — not dreamed, and it is the more foolish because it is no dream, because dreams excuse the fantasticalness."

Halfpenny said, "Then ask my bedfellow, you know him, who dreamt that night that the king of diamonds was sick."

In this society, it was common for unrelated people of the same sex to sleep in the same bed.

The three dreams were about food, the law, and playing cards.

Mother Bombie said, "But thy years and humors — thy age and disposition — pretty child, are subject to such fancies, which the more unsensible they seem, the more fantastical they are — the more unlike the real world they seem, the more fantastic they are — and so therefore this dream is easy to interpret.

"To children this is given from the gods:

"To dream of milk, fruit, babies [dolls], and rods.

"They betoken nothing [the dreams mean nothing] except that wantons must have rods."

In other words: Bad children must be beaten.

"Ten to one thy dream is true," Dromio said to Halfpenny. "Thou will be beaten."

Rixula said, "Gammer, I ask you to tell me who stole my spoon out of the buttery."

A "gammer" is a grandmother. The word could be used as a courtesy title to address someone who was not the speaker's biological grandmother.

A "buttery" is a pantry in which provisions such as butter and bread and ale were kept.

Mother Bombie said:

"Thy spoon is not stolen but mislaid,

"Thou are an ill huswife [housekeeper] though a good maid,

"Look for thy spoon where thou had like to be no maid."

In other words: Look for the spoon in that place where thou were likely to cease being a maiden, aka virgin.

"By the body of me, let me fetch the spoon," Rixula said. "I remember the place."

Lucio said, "Go slowly swift to the place. If the place is there now, it will be there tomorrow."

A proverb stated: "Make haste slowly."

Sometimes doing something swiftly results in making mistakes that take much time to fix.

Rixula said, "Aye, the place will be there, but perhaps the spoon will not."

Halfpenny asked, "Were thou once put to it?"

In other words: Did someone ask her to steal the spoon?

Rixula replied, "No, sir boy, it was put to me."

In other words: Someone had propositioned her.

"How was it missed?" Lucio asked

He meant the spoon, but Dromio punned on "missed" and took "it" to mean Rixula's virginity.

Dromio said:

"I'll guess for lack of a mist to hide her ugly face.

"But what's my fortune, mother?"

Mother Bombie said:

"Thy father does live because he does dye,

"Thou have spent all thy thrift with a die,

"And so like a beggar thou shall die."

Dromio's father dyed cloth for a living, and Dromio lost all his money gambling with dice.

Risio said, "I would have liked it well if all the gerunds had been there, -di, -do, and -dum, but to have all in 'die,' that's too deadly."

The endings of Latin gerunds are -di, -do, and -dum.

Dromio said, "My father indeed is a dyer, but I have been a dicer, but to die a beggar, give me permission not to believe Mother Bombie, and yet it may be true.

"I have nothing to live by except knavery, and if the world would grow honest, I would welcome beggary."

He made his living through trickery, but if he could not make his living that way, a suitable occupation for him would be begging.

Dromio then asked:

"But what have thou to say, Risio?"

"Nothing until I see whether all this that she has said is true," Risio said.

Halfpenny said to Dromio, "Aye, Risio would like to see thee beg."

Risio said, "Mother, tell us this: What are all our fortunes? We are engaging in a matter of legerdemain. How will it fodge — work out?"

Mother Bombie said:

"You shall all thrive like cheaters.

"That is, to be cheated by cheaters.

"All shall end well, and you shall be found to be cheaters."

Dromio said:

"Many thanks, Mother Bombie.

"We are all pleased, if you were for your pains."

Everyone will be pleased, if Mother Bombie is pleased with telling fortunes for no reward other than personal satisfaction. In her case, it would be the personal satisfaction of being right.

"I take no money, but I do take good words," Mother Bombie said. "Don't rail at and criticize me if I tell the truth. If I do not tell the truth, then take revenge on me. Farewell."

Mother Bombie shut the door of her house.

Dromio said, "Now we have nothing to do but to go about this business. Let Candius put on Accius' apparel, and I will array Accius with Candius' clothes."

Candius and Accius would impersonate each other.

Risio said:

"Here is Silena's attire. Lucio, put it upon Livia, and give me Livia's clothing for Silena to put on."

Silena and Livia would impersonate each other.

Risio continued:

"Once this is done, let Candius and Livia come forth, and let Dromio and me alone for the rest — leave it to Dromeo and me to do what is needed."

"What shall become of Accius and Silena?" Halfpenny asked.

Dromio replied, "Bah, their turn shall be next. All must be done in an orderly fashion. Let's get to it, for now it works."

They exited.

CHAPTER 4

— 4.1 —

Candius and Livia talked together.

Livia was dressed as the simpleton Silena, and Candius was dressed as the simpleton Accius.

Livia (dressed as Silena) said:

"This attire is very fit."

The clothing fit her well and was of better quality than she was accustomed to wear.

Livia (dressed as Silena) added:

"But what if this clothing should make me a fool and my clothing shall make Silena wise? You will then woo me and wed her."

Candius (dressed as Accius) said, "Thou know that Accius is also a fool, and his raiment fits me, so that if apparel is infectious, I am also likely to be a fool, and he is likely to be wise. What would be the conclusion? I wonder."

Dromio and Risio entered the scene.

Dromio was the serving-boy of Memphio, and Risio was the serving-boy of Stellio.

Memphio and Stellio wanted their children, Accius and Silena, both of whom were simpletons, to wed each other. Neither Memphio nor Stellio knew that the other's child was a simpleton.

"Here come our counselors," Livia (dressed as Silena) said.

"Well said," Dromio said. "I perceive that turtledoves fly in couples — in pairs."

"Else how should they couple and mate?" Risio asked.

"So do knaves go double, in twos; else how should they be so cunning in doubling," Livia (dressed as Silena) said.

"Doubling" means trickery.

"*Bona verba*, Livia," Candius (dressed as Accius) said.

In other words: Speak good words, Livia. Don't be overly critical.

Dromio said, "I understand Latin; that means that Livia is a good word."

Candius (dressed as Accius) said, "No, I told her to use good words."

"And what deeds do you tell her to do?" Risio asked.

"None but a deed of gift," Candius (dressed as Accius) said.

"What gift?" Risio asked.

"The gift of her heart," Candius (dressed as Accius) said.

Dromio said, "Give me permission to pose a question to you although you are a graduate, for I tell you that we in Rochester spur so many hackneys that we must necessarily spur scholars, for we take them for hackneys."

They spur horses, and they spur scholars. They spur scholars to engage in discussion by asking questions.

Livia (dressed as Silena) asked, "Why so, sir boy?"

Dromio said, "Because I knew two scholars hired for ten groats apiece to say service on Sunday, and that's no more than the cost to hire a post horse from here to Canterbury," Dromio said.

Scholars and post horses can be hired for the same amount of money.

"He knows what he says, for he once served the post-master," Risio said.

Candius (dressed as Accius) said, "Indeed, I think he served some post to his master. But come, Dromio, post me."

"Post me" means "post after me" or "come after me."

In other words: test me with your wit by asking me questions.

Dromio said, "You say you would have her heart for a deed."

"Well," Candius (dressed as Accius) said.

Dromio said:

"If you take her heart for *cor*, that heart in her body, then know this, *Molle eius levibus, cor enim inviolabile telis*. A woman's heart is thrust through with a feather."

The Latin means: My heart is soft and tender, and it is easily pierced by the arrow."

The arrow is Cupid's.

Dromio continued:

"If you mean she should give a hart named *cervus*, then you are worse, for *cornua cervus habet*, that is, to have one's heart grow out at his head, which will make one ache at the heart in their body."

Cervus is Latin for a hart: a male deer that is over five years old.

Cornua cervus habet is Latin for "a hart has horns."

Dromio was joking that Livia would give Candius the horns of a cuckold, and he would grieve at the heart because he had an unfaithful wife.

Sperantus and Prisius entered the scene.

Sperantus was the father of Candius, and Prisius was the father of Livia.

Each father did not want his child to marry the other father's child.

Livia (dressed as Silena), said, "I curse your harts and hearts. I hear someone coming. I know it is my father by the way he walks."

"What must we do?" Candius (dressed as Accius) asked.

Dromio said, "Why, do as I told you, and let me alone with the old men. Leave the old men to me, and you two get on with your marriage."

"Come, neighbor, I perceive the love of our children grows key cold," Prisius said.

"As cold as a key" means "extremely cold." Keys are made of metal, which can get very hot or very cold very quickly. Metals are good conductors of heat, and metals heat up and cool off quickly.

"I think it was never but lukewarm," Sperantus said.

Prisius said, "Bavins will have their flashes, and youth will have their fancies, the one is as quickly quenched as the other is burnt."

"Bavins" are bundles of brushwood that burn up quickly.

Prisius then asked, looking at the disguised Candius and the disguised Livia:

"But who are these two?"

Candius (dressed as Accius) said to Livia, "Here I plight my faith, taking thee for the staff of my age, and for the solace of my youth."

Livia (dressed as Silena) said to Candius, "And I vow to thee affection that nothing can dissolve, neither the length of time, nor the malice of fortune, nor the distance of place."

Candius and Livia were now legally betrothed. This was legally binding in common law; however, a church wedding still needed to be performed.

Therefore, Candius (dressed as Accius) asked Livia, "But when shall we be married in church?"

Livia (dressed as Silena) said to Candius, "That's a good question, for that one delay in wedding brings a hundred dangers in the Church. We will not be asked, and a license is too chargeable — too expensive — and to tarry until tomorrow is too tedious."

A delay in holding the church wedding would be frowned on by the ecclesiastical authorities. The couple did not want to wait for the banns: The announcement of the upcoming wedding each week for three weeks before the wedding was held. (The announcement of the banns was known as "asking." As part of the banns, anyone who had an objection to the wedding was asked to make that objection known.) The couple did not even want to wait until the next day for a formal wedding.

Dromio said, "There's a girl who stands on pricks until she is married."

Livia was very eager to marry. It was if she were standing on thorns in her bare feet.

Candius (dressed as Accius) said to Livia, "To avoid danger, charge and expense, and tediousness, let us now conclude it in the nearest church."

They wanted to get the blessing of a priest.

"Agreed," Livia (dressed as Silena) said.

Prisius and Sperantus had witnessed the betrothal of their children, and they had not recognized their children because of the clothing in which they were dressed.

"Who are these who hasten so to marry?" Prisius asked.

Dromio said, "By the Virgin Mary, sir, they are Accius, the son of Memphio, and Silena, the daughter of Stellio."

Sperantus said to Prisius, "I am sorry, neighbor, for our purposes are disappointed and frustrated."

Sperantus, the father of Candius, had wanted his son to marry Silena.

Prisius, the father of Livia, had wanted his daughter to marry Accius.

"You see that marriage is destiny, made in heaven, though consummated on earth," Prisius said.

"How do you like them?" Risio asked. "Aren't they a pretty couple?"

"Yes," Prisius said. "May God give them joy, seeing in spite of our hearts — our desires — they must join in marriage."

Dromio said, "I am sure that you are not angry, seeing that things already past cannot be recalled, and being witnesses to their contract, and so I am sure that you will be also well-willers to the match."

"For my part, I wish them well," Sperantus said.

"And so do I," Prisius said, "and since there is no remedy for my disappointed hopes, I am glad for their marriage."

Risio asked, "But will you never hereafter take it in dudgeon and be angry about it, but treat them as well as though you yourselves had made the marriage?"

Prisius said, "I will never be angry about this marriage."

"Nor will I," Sperantus said.

Dromio said to Candius (dressed as Accius), "Sir, here are two old men who are glad that your loves so long continued, are now so happily concluded."

Candius (dressed as Accius) said:

"We thank them, and if they will come to Memphio's house, they shall take part of a bad dinner."

"Dinner" was eaten in the late morning: It was the first big meal of the day.

Since he was still pretending to be Accius, Memphio's son, he invited them to a celebratory dinner. Calling it "a bad dinner" was a show of modesty.

He then whispered:

"This cottons, and it works like wax in a sow's ear."

"Cottons" means "is working out well," and "works like wax in a sow's ear" means "this is easy."

Candius (dressed as Accius) and Livia (dressed as Silena) exited.

Prisius said, "Well, seeing that the marriages we wanted have been prevented, we must lay other plots, for Livia shall not have Candius."

"Fear not, for I have sworn that Candius shall not have Livia," Sperantus said. "But let us not fall out and argue because our children fall in love together."

"Will thou go soon to Memphio's house?" Prisius asked.

Sperantus said, "Aye, and if you will, let us go together so that we may see how the young couple bride it — act as a married couple — and so we may teach our own children how to act."

They exited.

— 4.2 —

Lucio and Halfpenny talked together.

Lucio said, "By this time, I am sure, the wags have played their parts, and so there remains nothing now for us but to match Accius and Silena."

In other words: By this time, Dromio and Risio have gotten Candius and Livia married, and so now we — Halfpenny and I — need to get Accius and Silena married.

Halfpenny said:

"It was too good to be true, for we should laugh heartily, and without laughing, my spleen would split, but hush, here comes the man."

Accius entered the scene, coming from Memphio's house. He was dressed in Candius' clothing.

Halfpenny added:

"And yonder comes the maiden."

Silena entered the scene, coming from Stellio's house. She was dressed in Livia's clothing.

Halfpenny then said to Lucio:

"Let us stand to the side and watch and listen and comment."

They stood in a place where Accius and Silena could not easily see them.

Not seeing anyone else, Accius (dressed as Candius) said to himself, "What does my father mean to thrust me forth in another boy's coat? I'll warrant it is to as much purpose as a hen in the forehead."

A proverb about thinness stated, "As fat as a hen in the forehead."

A fathead is a stupid person.

Halfpenny whispered to Lucio, "There was an ancient proverb knocked in the head."

Accius (dressed as Candius) said, "I am almost come into my nonage, and yet I never was so far as the proverbs of this city."

"Nonage" means the time of immaturity and youth. Actually, he was about to leave the chronological age of immaturity and youth and enter the chronological age of an adult.

Instead of "proverbs," Accius should have said "suburbs."

"There's a quip for the suburbs of Rochester," Lucio whispered to Halfpenny.

"Excellently applied," Halfpenny said.

Not seeing anyone else, Silena (dressed as Livia) said to herself, "Well, although this apparel makes me a sullen and dull dame, yet I hope in my own apparel I am no saint."

Apparently, Silena thought that saints are sullen and dull.

Halfpenny whispered to Lucio, "A brave and splendid fight is likely to be between a cock with a long comb, and a hen with a long leg."

A cock with a long comb is a coxcomb: a fool. That, of course, is a male fool: Accius.

A hen with one long leg and one short leg will walk oddly. Yes, hens can become lame. The hen, of course, is a female fool: Silena.

But Halfpenny may have meant simply that Silena had long legs; after all, Silena is attractive.

"Her wits are shorter than her legs," Lucio whispered to Halfpenny.

"And his comb is longer than his wit," Halfpenny whispered to Lucio.

Seeing Silena, Accius (dressed as Candius) said:

"I have yonder uncovered a fair girl."

In hunting, "uncover" means to drive a bird or animal out from cover.

"Uncovered a fair girl." Hmm. Bawdy, that.

Accius then said to himself, "I'll be so bold as to spur her and ask her questions."

Accius then asked Selena, "What might a body call her name?"

Silena (dressed as Livia) said, "I cannot help you at this time. I ask you to come again tomorrow."

Halfpenny whispered to Lucio, "Aye, by the Virgin Mary, sir."

In other words, his interpretation of Silena's words were "So much for you, sir."

Accius (dressed as Candius) said to Silena, "You need not be so lusty. You are not so honest."

Lustful people may not be honest, aka chaste, but the word "lusty" at this time could mean "arrogant."

Silena (dressed as Livia) replied, "I beg your mercy. I took you for a joint stool."

A joint stool was made from a few pieces of wood joined together.

Lucio whispered to Halfpenny, "Here's courting for a conduit or a bakehouse."

A conduit was a place where people could get water and carry it home; it was a place where people gossiped. A bakehouse was another place where lower-class people gathered and gossiped.

The language that Accius and Selena were using was common, not refined.

Silena (dressed as Livia) said, "But what kind of man are you? I think you look as pleases God."

A proverb stated, "God makes and apparel shapes, but money makes the man."

Accius was wearing Candius' clothing, which was less good than his own clothing.

Accius (dressed as Candius) asked, "What! Do you give me the boots?"

"To give someone the boots" meant "to make fun of them."

Halfpenny whispered to Lucio, "Whether they will or will not get married, here are very good cobblers' cuts."

Cobblers cut out pieces of leather with which to make shoes, and Accius and Silena were verbally cutting each other.

The pieces of leather that cobblers cut out were then fit and sewed together. Accius and Silena seemed to fit together: They were very alike.

Accius (dressed as Candius) said, "I am taken with a fit of love: Have you thought about marriage?"

Silena (dressed as Livia) said, "I had thought to have asked you."

Accius (dressed as Candius) asked Silena, "Upon what acquaintance?"

People ought to be acquainted before they propose marriage to each other.

Silena (dressed as Livia) said, "Who would have thought it?"

"It" may mean "that we could be married."

Being in disguise can be a hindrance to becoming acquainted — and to proposing marriage.

Accius (dressed as Candius) said, "Much in my gaskins, more in my round hose. All my father's gaskins and hose are as white as daisies, and all my father's gaskins and hose are as full of meat as an egg."

Gaskins were loose-fitting trousers, and round hose were tightly fitting hose.

His father's gaskins and hose were often full of meat: his father's legs.

Earlier, Halfpenny had said, "A wren's egg is as full of meat as a goose egg, although there is not as much in it."

Possibly, Accius' response to Silena's question "Who would have thought it?" is this:

I would have thought it while wearing gaskins, and I would have thought it more while wearing round hose that fit more tightly and intimately. And my father would have thought it whatever he was wearing.

Certainly, his father, Memphio, did want Accius and Livia to be married. And for now, so did Accius.

Silena (dressed as Livia) said, "And all my father's plate is made of crimson velvet."

Plate is silverplate or goldplate. It is not made of red velvet cloth.

"Make," however, can mean "paired with."

Accius (dressed as Candius) said, "That's brave — excellent — with bread."

The bread is on the red velvet cloth, which is on the plate.

The point is that different things can be paired, matched, and mated.

Halfpenny whispered, "These three had 'wise' men as their fathers."

"These three" may be Accius, Silena, and Memphio (Accius' father).

According to Halfpenny, all three of these people are fools.

"Why?" Lucio whispered.

Halfpenny whispered, "Because when their bodies were at work about household stuff, their minds were busied about commonwealth matters."

Accius (dressed as Candius) gestured to a part of Silena's clothing and said, "This is pure lawn: fine linen. What do you call this? A preface to your hair?"

A "preface" can be a part of the ceremony of the Eucharist that offers praise and thanks to God. Accius may be saying that this part of Silena's clothing accentuates her hair.

Silena (dressed as Livia) said, "Wisely, you have picked a raisin out of a frail — a basket — of figs."

He had picked out one part of her clothing for special praise.

Accius (dressed as Candius) said, "Take it as you wish. You are in your own clothes."

Silena could take the praise well, or she could regard it as criticism of the rest of her clothing.

Silena (dressed as Livia) said, "Saving a reverence, but that's a lie. My clothes are better. My father borrowed these clothes I am wearing."

"Saving [a person's] reverence, but ..." means "I'm sorry, but ...."

Accius (dressed as Candius) said:

"Long may he so do: borrow clothing for you to wear."

Accius was complimenting what she was wearing.

Accius (dressed as Candius) continued:

"I could tell you that these clothes I am wearing are not mine if I would blab it like a woman."

"I would be as glad if you should tell them it snowed," Silena (dressed as Livia) said.

In other words: She doesn't much care for either alternative: wearing borrowed clothing, or enduring cold and snowy weather.

"Come, let us take them off, for we have had the cream of them," Lucio whispered to Halfpenny.

Hmm. It sounds as if he wanted to take off the clothing of Accius and Silena.

Another meaning of "take them off" is "separate them."

Halfpenny whispered to Lucio, "I'll guarantee that if this is the cream, then the milk is very flat. Let us join issue — start a debate — with them."

Lucio whispered:

"To have such issues — such children — of our bodies, is worse than to have an issue in the body."

This kind of issue is an oozing ulcer.

Lucio then said out loud to Silena:

"May God save you, pretty mouse."

Silena (dressed as Livia) said, "You may command and go without."

A proverb stated, "Ask and have."

Silena's version of the proverb was "Ask and have not."

Halfpenny whispered to Lucio:

"There's a gleek for you; let me have my gird."

A gleek is a jest.

A gird is a gibe: an insult.

Halfpenny then asked Silena out loud:

"On thy conscience, tell me what time it is."

Silena (dressed as Livia) said, "I beg your mercy. I have killed your cushion."

To "miss the cushion" means to "miss the mark" or to "make a mistake."

Both Silena and Accius misremembered and misused proverbial sayings.

Silena may be apologizing for not knowing what time it is.

Halfpenny said, "I am paid — mortally wounded by your remark — and struck dead in the nest. I am sure this soft youth who is not half as wise as you are fair, nor you altogether as fair as he is foolish, will not be so captious."

He was saying that both Silena and Accius were fools.

By "captious," Halfpenny meant that Silena and Accius would not cavil: They would not make petty objections to what would be proposed to them.

Accius (dressed as Candius) said, "Your eloquence surpasses my understanding."

Memphio and Stellio entered the scene from different directions. They did not see each other at first, and the others in the scene did not see them at first.

Lucio said, "I never heard that before, but shall we two make a marriage match between you?"

Silena (dressed as Livia) said about Accius, "I'll know first who was his father."

Accius (dressed as Candius), "My father? Why do you need to care about him? I hope he was not your father."

Halfpenny whispered to Lucio, "A hard question, for it is a good bet that one father begat both of them. He who cut out the upper leather also cut out the inner, and so with one awl he stitched two soles together."

Hmm. An awl pierces holes.

The hypothetical father may have stitched two souls together.

The two fathers, Memphio and Stellio, had plots of their own afoot.

Memphio was the father of Accius, and Stellio was the father of Silena.

Each father was looking at the back of his own child, did not recognize his own child, and so would inquire about him or her. Each father would not recognize his own child until he or she turned around and faced him.

Dromio had told Memphio that someone would meet Stellio's daughter and would court her while impersonating Memphio's son: Accius.

Risio had told Stellio that someone would meet Memphio's son and would plead — encourage a betrothal — while impersonating Stellio's daughter: Silena.

Stellio got the attention of Lucio, Memphio's serving-boy, and whispered, referring to Silena, "Who is she?"

"She is Prisius' daughter," Halfpenny answered.

Prisius' daughter is Livia, whose clothing Silena was wearing.

Stellio said to himself, "The plan is fodging in good time — is working in good time."

Memphio got the attention of Halfpenny, Stellio's serving-boy, and whispered about Accius, "Who is he?"

Halfpenny whispered, "Sperantus' son."

Sperantus' son is Candius, whose clothing Accius was wearing.

Memphio said to himself, "Good. It will cotton: It will work out."

Accius (dressed as Candius) asked Silena, "Damsel, please tell me how old you are."

Memphio said to himself, "My son would scarcely have asked such a foolish question."

Accius, Memphio's son, would definitely have asked such a foolish question, and Memphio knew it. By "my son," Memphio meant "the person impersonating my son." That person was not supposed to be foolish.

Silena (dressed as Livia) replied, "I shall be eighteen next bear-baiting."

Bear-baiting was a cruel sport in which dogs tormented a chained bear.

Stellio said to himself, "My daughter would have made a wiser answer."

Silena, Stellio's daughter, would definitely not have made a wiser answer, and Stellio knew it. By "my daughter," Stellio meant "the person impersonating my daughter." That person was not supposed to be foolish.

Halfpenny whispered to Lucio, "O how fitly this comes off!"

He was entertained by what he was seeing and hearing.

Accius (dressed as Candius) said, "My father is a scold. What's yours?"

Memphio said, "My heart throbs, I will look him in the face, and yonder I see Stellio!"

Stellio also noticed Memphio for the first time as he said to himself, "My mind misgives me, but hush, yonder is Memphio."

Seeing his father, Accius (dressed as Candius) said, "In faith I perceive an old and rusty saw: no fool to the old fool."

A saw is a proverbial saying.

He meant: There is no fool comparable to the old fool.

Accius (dressed as Candius) then asked his father, Memphio:

"I ask you why I was thrust out like a scare crow in this similitude."

By "similitude," Accius may have meant 1) multitude, and 2) disguise (similarity to Candius).

Recognizing Accius, Memphio said to himself, "My son! And I am shamed! Dromio shall die."

Seeing Stellio, Silena (dressed as Livia) said to him, "Father, are you sneaking behind? I ask you what must I do next?"

Recognizing Silena, Stellio said to himself, "My daughter! Risio, thou have cheated me."

"Now begins the game," Lucio said.

"How did you come to be here?" Memphio asked Accius.

Accius (dressed as Candius) answered, "By the Virgin Mary, by the way from your house hither."

True, but not an answer to the question Memphio wanted to be answered.

Memphio asked Accius, "How does it happen that you are in this attire?"

Accius (dressed as Candius) asked, "How does it happen that Dromio told me to put on this attire?"

Memphio said to himself, "Ah, thy son will be begged for a concealed fool."

He was worried that someone would get custody of Accius after he — Memphio — died and so would control the estate that Accius would inherit.

Accius (dressed as Candius) said, "Will I? Indeed, sir, no."

Stellio asked his daughter, Silena, "Why did you come here, Silena, without permission?"

Silena (dressed as Livia) said, "Because I did, and I am here because I am."

True, but not an answer to the question Stellio wanted to be answered.

Stellio said, "Poor wench, thy wit is improved to the uttermost."

In other words: Silena was as intelligent as she was going to get.

The word "improved," in addition to meaning "developed," can also mean "raised," as in the developing — that is, the raising — of rent.

Using the second definition of "improved," Halfpenny said, "Aye, it is a hard matter to have a wit of the old rent, everyone racks his commons so high — that is, charges more."

Memphio said to himself, "Dromio told me that someone would meet Stellio's daughter, and court her while impersonating my son: Accius."

Stellio said to himself, "Risio told me that someone would meet Memphio's son and plead — encourage a betrothal — while impersonating my daughter: Silena."

"But alas, I see that my son has himself met with Silena, and he has revealed his folly," Memphio said to himself.

"But I see that my daughter has prattled with Accius, and he has discovered her simplicity," Stellio said to himself.

Lucio said to Halfpenny, "A brave cry to hear the two old mules weep over the young fools."

"Accius, how do thou like Silena?" Memphio asked.

Accius (dressed as Candius) replied, "I take her to be pregnant."

The word "pregnant" can mean "pregnant with wit" as well as "pregnant with child."

Silena (dressed as Livia) said, "Truly his talk is very personable."

The word "personable" can mean 1) "pleasing in appearance," or 2) "pleasing in manner."

Apparently, Accius and Silena did not regard each other as fools.

Stellio said to Silena, "Come inside, girl, this business must be fetched about — it must be considered from another direction."

Memphio said, "Come, Accius, let us go inside."

Lucio said, "Sir, there is no harm done. They have neither bought nor sold: They haven't committed themselves to anything. They may be twins for their wits and years."

Both Accius and Silena were young fools.

Memphio asked, "But why did thou tell me it was Prisius' son?"

"Because I thought thee a fool to ask who thine own son was," Halfpenny replied.

Halfpenny was Sperantus' serving-boy, not Memphio's serving-boy, and so Halfpenny spoke frankly to Memphio.

Lucio said to Stellio, "And so, sir, as for your daughter, education has done much; otherwise, they are by nature soft witted enough."

He was sarcastic about Silena's education: In this society, many girls and women were not educated.

Memphio said, "Alas, their joints are not yet tied; they are not yet come to years and discretion."

He was saying that they were still young — too young to know discretion.

"Their joints are not yet tied" means "their joints are not yet knitted together."

Accius (dressed as Candius) asked, "Father, if my hands were to be tied up, shall I grow wise?"

"Aye, and Silena will be wise, too, if you tie your hands fast to your tongues," Halfpenny said.

Silena (dressed as Livia) said, "You may take your pleasure of my tongue, for it is no man's wife."

An unintended meaning of her words was that Halfpenny could use her tongue sexually.

"Come inside, Accius," Memphio said.

Stellio said, "Come inside, Silena. I will talk with Memphio's son, Accius. But as for Risio —"

He wanted to punish Risio, his serving-boy.

Memphio said, "As for Dromio —"

He wanted to punish Dromio, his serving-boy.

Memphio and Accius went inside Memphio's house.

Stellio and Silena went inside Stellio's house.

Halfpenny said, "Ass for you, all four!"

He was calling all four of them asses: fools.

Dromio and Risio entered the scene.

Dromio said, "How goes the world? Now we have made all sure: Candius and Livia are married, and their fathers are consenting, yet they do not know what they have consented to."

Lucio said:

"We have completely marred everything.

"As Accius and Silena courted one another, their fathers took them napping — unawares. Both fathers are ashamed, and you both shall be beaten."

Risio said:

"Tush, let us alone and leave it to us. We will persuade them that all falls out for the best, for if this marriage match had been concluded underhand — by secret means — they both would have been cheated, and now seeing they find both to be fools, they may be both — both sets of fools — better advised and act more wisely."

Both children would have been cheated because they would have married a fool, and both fathers would have been cheated because their children would have married a fool.

Memphio and Stellio were fools, and Accius and Silena were fools.

Risio then asked:

"But why is Halfpenny so sad?"

Halfpenny answered, "Because I am sure I shall never be a penny."

Risio said, "You should rather pray that there be no fall in the value of money, for thou will then go for a q."

A q is a farthing. If Halfpenny were to be worth a farthing, his value would fall by half. Instead of being worth half of a penny, he would be worth a quarter of a penny.

Dromio asked, "But didn't the two fools currently court one another?"

Current coinage is legal tender.

Current courting is smoothly running courting.

Lucio said, "These are very good words fitly applied, brought in, in the nick of time — the exact, right time."

A hackneyman and a sergeant entered the scene.

A hackneyman hires out horses and/or hackney carriages, and a sergeant has the power to arrest people.

The sergeant said to Dromio, "I arrest you."

"Me, sir?" Dromio asked. "Why then didn't you bring a stool with thee, so that I might sit down?"

"Arrest," in a pun, is "a rest."

The hackneyman said, "He arrests you at my suit for a horse."

He meant that the sergeant was arresting Dromio over the matter of a horse.

Risio deliberately misinterpreted "arrests you [Dromio] ... for a horse" to mean "arrest you [Dromio], who are a horse."

Risio said, "The more ass he — if he had arrested a mare instead of a horse, it would have been only a slight oversight, but to arrest a man who has no likeness of a horse, is flat lunacy or ale-acy."

"Ale-acy" is lunacy brought on by drinking too much ale.

The hackneyman said, "Bah, I hired him a horse."

He meant that he had rented Dromio a horse.

Dromio said, "I swear then he was well ridden."

The hackneyman said, "I think in two days he was never baited."

"Baited" means 1) fed, or 2) tormented, as in bear-baiting.

Halfpenny asked, "Why, was it a bear thou ride on?"

"I mean he never gave him bait," the hackneyman said.

"Bait" can also mean a lure to catch fish.

"Why, he took him for no fish," Lucio said.

The hackneyman said:

"I mistake none of you when I take you for fools."

He then said to Dromio:

"I say thou never gave my horse meat."

"Meat" is food.

Dromio said, "Yes, in four and forty hours, I am sure he had a bottle — a portion — of hay as big as his belly."

The sergeant said, "Nothing else? Thou should have given him provender."

"Provender" is horse feed.

"Why, he never asked for any," Risio said.

The hackneyman asked, "Why, do thou think a horse can speak?"

"No, for I spurred him until my heels ached, and he never said a word," Dromio said.

The hackneyman said, "Well, thou shall pay sweetly for spoiling him. It was as lusty and vigorous a nag as any in Rochester, and one that would stand upon no ground."

According to the hackneyman, the horse was so full of energy that it wouldn't stand still.

Dromio said, "Then he is as good as he ever was, I'll warrant. He'll do nothing but lie down."

According to Dromio, the horse wouldn't stand up.

The hackneyman said, "I lent him to thee gently — with good will."

Dromio said, "And I restored him so gently — in such a gentle and quiet state — that he neither would cry 'whinny,' nor would he wag the tail."

A proverb stated, "It is an ill horse that can neither whinny nor wag his tail."

The hackneyman asked, "But why did thou bore him thorough the ears?"

Having a hole bored through a horse's ears was a way of making identification and ownership of a horse easy to determine. The hackneyman's implication was that Dromio was going to claim ownership of the horse and sell it.

"It may be that the horse was set in the pillory because he had not a true pace," Lucio said.

An extra punishment for those in a pillory was to have holes put in their ears.

Halfpenny said, "No, it was for tiring."

The word "tiring" can mean "nagging."

The hackneyman said, "He would never tire, but it may be he would be so weary that he would go no further, or some such reason."

Dromio said, "Yes, he was a notable horse for service; he would tire and retire."

"Service" can mean 1) work, and 2) military service.

"Retire " can mean "retreat."

The hackneyman said:

"Do you think I'll be jested out of my horse?

"Sergeant, wreak and execute thy office on him."

"Wait," Risio said. "Let him be bailed."

"So he shall when I make a bargain with him," the hackneyman said.

Dromio said:

"It was a very good horse I must necessarily confess, and now listen to his qualities and have the patience to hear them since I must pay for him.

"He would stumble three hours in one mile."

A healthy person can walk one mile in fifteen minutes.

Dromio continued:

"I had thought I had rode upon adzes — sharp-edged tools — between this town of Rochester and the town of Canterbury.

"If one gave him water, why, he would lie down and bathe himself like a hawk.

"If one ran him, he would simper and mump — that is, look coy and mope — as though he had gone a wooing to a malt mare — a female dray horse — at Rochester.

"He trotted with his front legs and he ambled with his back legs, and he was so obedient that he would do duty and kneel like a dutiful son every minute on his knees, as though every stone had been his father."

"I am sure he had no diseases," the hackneyman said.

Dromio said, "He had a little rheum or pose, and he lacked nothing but a handkerchief."

"Rheum" is running of the eyes or nose, and "pose" is a head cold with running of the nose.

The sergeant said, "Come, what a tale of a horse have we here! I cannot stay. Thou must go with me to prison."

"If thou are a good fellow, hackneyman, take all our four bonds for the payment," Risio said. "Thou know we are town-born children, and we will not shrink the city for a pelting jade."

In other words: They were local residents, and they would not run out on their obligation because of a pelting — that is, poor-quality — horse.

Halfpenny said:

"I'll enter into a statute merchant to see it answered — to guarantee the repayment."

A statute merchant would allow the creditor to seize the debtor's property in case of default.

Halfpenny added:

"But if thou will have bonds, thou shall have a bushel full."

The hackneyman said:

"Alas, poor ant, thou bound in a statute merchant! A brown thread — a cheap bit of string — will bind thee fast enough."

The word "ant" was a reference to Halfpenny's small size.

The hackneyman added:

"But if all four of you will be content to jointly enter into a bond, I will withdraw the action."

Dromio said:

"Yes, I'll warrant that they will."

He asked his friends:

"What do you say?"

"I yield," Halfpenny said. "I'll do it."

"And I," Risio said.

"And I," Lucio said.

The hackneyman said, "Well, call the scrivener."

Scriveners drew up legal documents.

"Here's one nearby," the sergeant said. "I'll call him."

Risio said, "A scrivener's shop clings to a sergeant's mace like a burr clings to a frieze coat."

"Frieze" is woolen cloth.

A mace is a staff of office.

"What's the matter?" the scrivener asked.

"You must take a note of a bond — a legal agreement," the hackneyman said.

Dromio said, "A pint of courtesy pulls on a pot — a cup — of wine; in this tavern we'll dispatch and conclude the business."

"Agreed," the hackneyman said.

They would conclude the business with drinking.

Everyone but Risio went into the tavern.

Alone, Risio said to himself:

"Now if our wits are not in the wane, our knavery shall be at the full, for they — the serving-boys — will ride them — the hackneyman, the sergeant, and the scrivener — worse than Dromio rid his horse, for if the wine masters their wits, you shall see them bleed — show — their follies."

The serving-boys would end up mocking the hackneyman, the sergeant, and the scrivener.

One effect of wine is that excessive drinkers end up making fools of themselves and suffering for it.

Risio went into the tavern.

CHAPTER 5

— 5.1 —

Dromio, Risio, Lucio, and Halfpenny walked out of the tavern and talked together.

Dromio said, "Let every fox go to his hole; the hounds are at hand."

In other words: Let all us foxes leave and avoid the trouble.

Risio said, "The sergeant's mace lies at pawn for the reckoning — the paying of the bill — and he is under the board to cast it up."

The sergeant was drunk and under the table, where he was 1) casting — calculating — the bill, and/or 2) casting — vomiting — what he had drunk.

Lucio said, "The scrivener cannot keep his pen out of the pot; every goblet is an inkhorn."

The scrivener could not keep his pen — nose — out of the drinking pot — the drinking cup.

Halfpenny said:

"The hackneyman whisks with his wand — his whip — as if the tavern were his stable, and all the servants were his horses.

"He says, 'Jost there up, bay Richard,' and white loaves are horsebread — horse feed — in his eyes."

A joss-block was a mounting block, and so the hackneyman may have been imagining that he was telling a horse to go to the mounting block so the hackneyman could get on him.

Possibly, people in the tavern would understand "jost" — mount — to have a bawdy meaning.

Dromio said, "It is well I have my acquittance of debt, and he has such a bond of repayment that shall do him no more good than the bond of a faggot — a bundle of firewood. Our knaveries are now come to the push, and we must cunningly dispatch all."

The idiom "when push comes to shove" means "it is time for action: A critical point has been reached."

Now everything was rushing to a conclusion.

Dromio continued:

"We two — Risio and I — will go and see how we may appease our masters. You two go and see how you may conceal the recent marriage.

"If all fall out amiss, the worst thing that can happen is a beating. If all fall out to the best, the worst thing that can happen is liberty!"

Risio said, "Then let's go about it speedily, for so many irons in the fire together require a diligent plumber."

In this society, a plumber was a worker in metal.

They exited.

— 5.2 —

Vicinia talked to herself outside Mother Bombie's house:

"My heart throbs, my ears tingle, my mind misgives me since I hear such muttering of marriages in Rochester.

"My conscience, which for these eighteen years has been frozen with concealed guiltiness, begins now to thaw in open grief, but I will not accuse myself until I see more danger.

"The good old woman Mother Bombie shall try her cunning upon me, and if I perceive that my case is hopeless by her words, then I will come forward and confess what I have done, although with shame and hope to be forgiven, rather than report too late and have my actions be seen as inexcusable."

She knocked on Mother Bombie's door and when Mother Bombie opened it, Vicinia said:

"God speed, good mother."

This meant: May God help you succeed, good old woman."

Mother Bombie said, "Welcome, sister."

"Sister" and "mother" were complimentary titles.

Vicinia said:

"I am troubled in the night with dreams, and in the day with fears.

"My estate is laid bare, which I cannot well bear, but my practices are devilish, which I cannot call back and undo.

"If therefore in these aged years of yours, there is any deep skill, tell what my fortune shall be, and tell me what my fault and crime is."

Mother Bombie said:

"In studying to be overnatural,

"Thou are likely to be unnatural,

"And all about a natural.

"Thou shall be eased of a charge

"If thou thy conscience discharge,

"And this I commit to thy charge."

110

"Overnatural" means "trying to be too protective as a mother."

"Unnatural" means "going against nature, as in not doing what is most ethical and best for your children."

A "natural" is a fool.

Vicinia needs to relieve her conscience, which she can do by doing the right and ethical action. This is her charge: her responsibility.

Vicinia replied:

"Thou have touched me to the quick, mother.

"I understand thy meaning, and thou well know my practice, aka evil deed. I will follow thy counsel.

"But what will be the end? What will be the outcome?"

Mother Bombie said, "Thou shall know that before this day ends, and so, farewell."

Mother Bombie shut the door.

Vicinia said to herself:

"Now I perceive that I must either reveal an evil deed I have committed, or I must suffer a continual inconvenience."

The continual inconvenience would be a constant bad conscience for not revealing her bad deed and for not preventing the bad consequences that could follow from that bad deed.

Vicinia continued talking to herself:

"I must hasten homewards and resolve to make all whole. Better a little shame than an infinite grief. The strangeness — uncommonness — will abate and lessen the fault and crime, and revealing the bad deed will wipe it clean away."

Infinite grief is felt in Hell by unrepentant sinners.

— 5.3 —

Three fiddlers — Synis, Nasutus, and Beduneus — talked together.

Synis said, "Come, fellows, it is almost day. Let us have a fit of mirth and music at Sperantus' door and give a song to the bride."

Sperantus was the father of Candius, and Candius and Livia (the daughter of Prisius) had married. Sperantus and Prisius, however, did not know that their children had married. The father thought that Accius and Silena (whom Candius and Livia had been disguised as) had married.

The musicians, however, had heard that Candius and Livia were married.

"I believe they are asleep," Nasutus said. "It would be a pity to awaken them."

"It would be a shame they should sleep the first night," Beduneus said.

Newlyweds have better things to do than sleep.

"But who can tell at which house they lie," Synis said. "It may be that they are at Prisius' house. We'll try both houses."

"Come, let's draw like men," Nasutus said.

They would play their fiddles like men.

Warriors draw their swords out of their sheaths. Bows can be likened to swords.

Synis said:

"Now, tune; tune, I say."

Beduneus had some trouble tuning.

Synis complained:

"That boy, I think, will never profit in his faculty: He will never do well as a fiddler. He loses his rosin and so his fiddle goes cush, cush, a sound like that made by someone going wetshod in wet shoes. And his mouth is so dry that he hasn't spittle for his pin as I have."

Rosin was used on bowstrings.

Spittle was used to moisten the holes in which tuning pegs, aka pins, were set; the spittle helped keep the fiddle in tune longer.

Beduneus said, "By the Virgin Mary, sir, you see I go wetshod and dry mouthed, for yet I could never get new shoes or good drink. Rather than lead this life, I will throw my fiddle into the leads for a hobbler."

According to the *Oxford English Dictionary*, "leads" are "strips of lead used to cover a roof," and a "lead" (singular) is "A path; a garden path; an alley."

A hobbler is a wobbling child's toy top.

Beduneus was threatening to throw away his fiddle because he could not get good notes out of it.

"Boy, no more words," Synis said. "There's a time for all things, although I say it who should not say it. I have been a minstrel these thirty years, and I have tickled more strings than thou have hairs, but I was never yet so misused."

"Let us not brabble — quarrel — but play," Nasutus said. "Tomorrow is a new day."

Beduneus said:

"I am sorry I speak in your cast — I am sorry to interrupt you.

"What shall we sing?"

Synis answered, "'The Love Knot,' for that's best for a bridal."

A bridal is a wedding feast. Or it is a wedding and the celebrations associated with it.

They sang the song.

Synis said, "Good morning, fair bride, and may God send you joy of your bridal."

Sperantus looked out of a window and said to himself:

"What a bad deed do the twanglers make here! We have no trenchers — no plates — to scrape. It makes my teeth on edge to hear such grating.

The twanglers are the singers.

Sperantus then told the singers:

"Get you packing, or I'll make you wear double stocks, and yet you shall be never the warmer."

The double stocks are not stockings; they are the two stocks of a pillory.

"We come for good will, to wish the bride and bridegroom that God give them joy," Synis said.

"Here is no wedding," Sperantus said.

"Yes, your son and Prisius' daughter, Livia, were married, although you seem not to know it, yet they do not repent their wedding, I am sure," Synis said.

Sperantus said, "My son, the villain! I would prefer that he had been fairly hanged."

He meant hung on a gallows.

Nasutus said, "So he is, sir; you have your wish."

He meant "well hung."

Candius came out of his father's house and said quietly to the musicians:

"Here, fiddlers, take this money and don't say a word."

He gave the fiddlers money and then said loudly so his father would hear:

"Here is no wedding. It was at Memphio's house, yet I give you great thanks. Your music, although it missed the house, hit and pleased the mind. We were making our wedding preparations."

Candius and Livia were married, but Candius did not want to reveal that just yet, so he was pretending that Accius and Silena were married, although they were not.

Synis said to Sperantus, "I beg your mercy, sir. I think it was Memphio's son who was married."

Memphio's son was Accius.

"O ho, the case is altered," Sperantus said. "Go thither then and be haltered for me."

"Haltered" means "hung."

"What's the alms?" Nasutus asked. "How much did Candius give us?"

"An angel," Synis said.

An angel was a gold coin worth ten shillings. This was a very good tip.

Beduneus said:

"I'll warrant there's some work towards: some plot afoot.

"Ten shillings is real money, even in Master Mayor's purse."

Even a rich man such as the mayor would find an angel to be a significant amount of money.

"Let us go to Memphio's house and share equally," Synis said. "When we have finished, all of you shall have new shoes."

Beduneus said, "Aye, such as they cry at the 'sizes, 'A mark in issues,' and 'mark in issues [his shoes],' and yet I never saw so much leather as would piece — patch — one's shoes.

The 'sizes are the Assizes, a session in which justice was administered.

"Mark in issues" is 1) a fine of a mark (a unit of money), and 2) a flaw in a shoe.

Synis said:

"No more joking."

He divided the money among them and said:

"There's the money."

Beduneus said, "A good handsel — a good beginning — and I think the maidenhead of your liberality. This is the first time you have been generous."

Nasutus said, "Come, here's Memphio's house. What shall we sing?"

Synis answered, "You know that Memphio is very rich and wise, and therefore let us strike the gentle stroke, and sing a catch."

All three fiddlers sang:

"*The bride this night can catch no cold,*

"*No cold, the bridegroom's young, not old,*
"*Like ivy he her fast does hold,*"
The first fiddler sang:
"*And clips her.*"
"Clips" means "embraces."
The second fiddler sang:
"*And lips her.*"
"Lips" means "kisses."
The third fiddler sang:
"*And flips her, too.*"

The bridegroom could flip the bride onto her stomach or back for a new sexual position. Or a "flip" could be a playful slap, perhaps on the bride's butt.

All three fiddlers sang:
"*Then let them alone,*
"*They know what they do.*"
The first fiddler sang:
"*At laugh and lie down, if they play,*"
The second fiddler sang:
"*What ass against the sport can bray?*"
The third fiddler sang:
"*Such tick-tack has held many a day,*"

"Tick-tack" is a game that involves the insertion of pegs into holes.

The first fiddler sang:
"*And longer.*"
The second fiddler sang:
"*And stronger.*
"*It still holds, too.*"
All three fiddlers sang:
"*Then let them alone,*
"*They know what they do,*
"*This night,*

"*In delight*
"*Does thump away sorrow.*
"*Of billing*
"*Take your filling,*
"*So good morrow, good morrow.*"

"Thump" means "beat."

"Billing" means "kissing."

"Morrow" means "morning."

Nasutus said, "Good morrow, mistress bride, and may God send you a huddle — an embrace."

Memphio, the father of Accius, said, "What crowding knaves have we there? Case up your fiddles, or the constable shall cage you up. What bride are you talking about?"

Synis said:

"Here has been a wedding in Rochester, and it was told to me first that Sperantus' son had married Prisius' daughter — that Candius had married Livia.

"We were there, and they sent us to your worship, saying your son was matched with Stellio's daughter — that Accius had married Silena."

Thinking that he was the victim of a practical joke, Memphio said, "Has Sperantus — that churl — nothing to do but mock his neighbors? I'll be even with him. And get yourselves gone, or I swear by the rood's body I'll lay you by the heels."

"The rood's body" is the body of Christ, crucified on a rood — a cross.

"To lay someone by the heels" means "to have someone arrested and put in the stocks."

Angry, Nasutus said:

"Sing a catch! Here's a fair catch indeed!

"Sing until we catch cold in our feet, and be called 'knave' until our ears glow on our heads.

"Your worship is 'wise,' sir."

Memphio said to his serving-boy, "Dromio, shake off — unleash — a whole kennel of officers, to punish these jarring rogues. I'll teach them to stretch their dried sheep's guts at my door, and to mock one who stands to be made mayor."

Dried sheep's guts were used to make bowstrings.

Memphio was hoping to become Mayor of Rochester.

Dromio said:

"I had thought they had been sticking of — killing — pigs because I heard such a squeaking.

"I go, sir."

Memphio and Dromio moved away from the window.

"Let us be packing," Synis said. "Let's go."

"Where is my scabbard?" Nasutus said. "Let everyone sheathe his science."

His "scabbard" was a fiddle case.

Struggling with putting his fiddle into its case, Beduneus said, "A plague on the shoemaker who made this boot — this case — for my fiddle. This case is too strait — too narrow."

Synis said:

"No more words. It will be thought the offenders were the four waits. Let them wring — let them suffer."

The four waits were four musicians maintained at public charge. They would be blamed instead of Synis, Nasutus, and Beduneus for causing a disturbance.

Synis continued:

"As for the wags who played this practical joke on us, we'll talk with them."

They exited.

— 5.4 —

Memphio and Dromio came out of Memphio's house.

"The musicians are gone, sir," Dromio said.

Memphio said:

"If they had stayed, the stocks would have stayed them."

They would have been put in the stocks, and they would not have been able to move.

Memphio then asked:

"But sirrah, what shall we do now?"

Dromio said, "As I advised you, make a marriage match, for it is better for one house to be encumbered with two fools than for two houses to be encumbered with two fools."

A proverb stated, "Two fools in one house are too many."

Memphio said:

"It is true, for it being bruited about that each of us has a fool, as a child, who, if the person is wise, will make an offer of marriage to any of them?"

Memphio was sure that because of gossip, everyone knew that his son and Stellio's daughter were fools.

Memphio continued:

"Besides, fools are fortunate, fools are fair, fools are honest."

A proverb stated, "A fool cannot speak unlike himself."

Dromio said:

"Aye, sir, and more than that, fools are not wise.

"A wise man is melancholy for moonshine in the water."

In other words: A wise man longs for something that is impossible to get.

Dromio continued:

"A wise man is full of worry, building castles in the air."

In other words: A wise man is anxious because he tries to do things that are impossible to do.

Dromio continued:

"A wise man commonly has a fool as his heir."

Memphio said, "But what do thou say to thy dame's chafing — thy mistress' fretting and nagging?"

Memphio had a shrewish wife.

"Nothing but that all her dishes are chafing dishes," Dromio said.

Chafing dishes keep food warm for a long time.

"I wish that her tongue were in thy belly," Memphio said.

This would accomplish two things: 1) silence his wife, and 2) feed Dromio.

"I would as willingly have a raw ox-tongue in my stomach," Dromio said.

He would prefer a different kind of food.

"Why?" Memphio asked.

Dromio said:

"The clapper of a bell makes my ears burn a quarter of a mile off.

Church bells are loud.

"By the Virgin Mary, imagine if the clapper — your wife's noisy tongue — were to hang within an inch of my heart. Don't you think it would beat my heart black and blue?"

Memphio said, "Well, patience is a virtue, but pinching is worse than any vice, I will break this matter to Stellio, and if he is willing, this day shall be their wedding."

He was now willing to permit his son, Accius, to marry Stellio's daughter, Silena.

"Then this day shall be my liberty!" Dromio said.

Memphio said, "Aye, if Stellio's daughter had been wise, and if by thy means she had been tricked into accepting a fool to be her husband."

Dromio said, "Then sir, I'll revolt, and dash out the brains of your devices. I'll ruin your plans."

"Rather than that, I shall allow thou to be free," Memphio said.

They exited.

— 5.5 —

Sperantus and his serving-boy, Halfpenny, entered the scene from one direction.

Prisius and his serving-boy, Lucio, entered the scene from another direction.

Sperantus said to Halfpenny:

"Boy, this smoke is a token of some fire. I don't like the luck of it. It seems like an ill omen.

"Why should these minstrels dream of a marriage?"

"Alas, sir, they rustle and creep into every place," Halfpenny said. "Give credit to no such words."

Sperantus said:

"I will go to Prisius. I cannot be quiet and at peace in my mind, and at a good time — now — I see and meet him."

He said to Prisius:

"Good morning, neighbor."

Prisius said, "I cast the morning in thy face, and I bid 'good night' to all the neighborhood."

Sperantus said:

"This is your old trick, to pick one's purse and then to pick quarrels.

"I tell thee, I had rather thou would rob my money chest than imbecile and embezzle my son."

"Embezzle" means "cheat."

To "imbecile" Sperantus' son, Candius, means to "marry him to a fool."

Prisius said:

"Thy son! My daughter is seduced, for I hear say she is married, and our serving-boys can tell."

He then said to his serving-boy, Lucio, "What do thou say? Tell the truth or I'll grind thee to powder in my mill. Are they married?"

Of course, Candius and Livia were in fact married.

"It is true that they were both in a church," Lucio said.

"That is no fault," Prisius said. "The place is holy."

"And there was with them a priest," Halfpenny said.

"Why, what place is fitter for a priest than a church?" Sperantus said.

"And they took one another by the hand," Lucio said.

"Bah, that's only common courtesy," Prisius said.

"And the priest spoke many kind words," Halfpenny said.

Prisius said:

"That showed he was no dumb minister."

"Dumb" can mean "unable to speak." Or the word may refer to a silenced clergyman — one not allowed to speak because of heterodox views not conforming with orthodox views.

Prisius added:

"But what did they say? Did thou hear any words between them?"

"Indeed, there was a bargain during life, and the clock cried, 'God give them joy,'" Lucio said.

Weddings at this time had to be performed before the clock struck twelve. The clock's striking after the wedding was performed showed that the wedding had been completed before twelve.

"Villain!" Prisius said. "They are married."

"Nay, I don't think so," Halfpenny said.

Sperantus said:

"Yes, yes, 'God give you joy' is a binder. It finishes the wedding ceremony.

"I'll quickly be resolved."

He called:

"Candius, come forth."

Candius came out of Sperantus' house.

Prisius said:

"And I'll be put out of doubt."

He called:

"Livia, come forth."

Livia came out of Prisius' house.

"The micher — the truant — hangs down his head," Sperantus said about his son, Candius.

"The baggage begins to blush," Prisius said about his daughter, Livia.

"Now the game begins," Halfpenny whispered to Lucio.

"I believe it will be no game for us," Lucio whispered back.

The two serving-boys could soon be in big trouble.

"Are you married, young master?" Sperantus asked his son.

"I cannot deny it," Candius replied. "It was done very recently."

"But thou shall repent that it was done so soon," Sperantus said.

"Then it is bootless — pointless — to ask you, Livia, if you are married," Prisius said.

"Aye, and it is needless to be angry," Livia said.

"It shall surpass anger," Prisius said. "Thou shall find it rage."

"You gave your consent," Livia said.

"Impudent giglot — hussy — wasn't it enough to abuse me?" Prisius asked. "Do you also have to lie about me?"

Candius said to his father, "You, sir, agreed to this marriage match."

Sperantus asked:

"Thou brazen-face boy, do thou think to use your learning to persuade me that I agreed to this marriage? Where did I consent? When did I consent? What witness says that I did consent?"

Candius said, "You consented in this place yesterday before Dromio and Risio."

Prisius said, "I remember that we heard a marriage contract between Memphio's son and Stellio's daughter, and that our good wills, which were not needed, being asked for, we gave them, which was of no significance."

Candius said, "It was only the apparel of Accius and Silena. We — Livia and I — were the persons in the apparel and the persons who made the marriage contract."

Realizing that he had agreed to the marriage, Prisius said:

"O villainy not to be borne!"

He then said to his serving-boy, Lucio:

"Were thou privy to this practice? Did you know about this trick?"

"In a manner," Lucio said.

"I'll pay thee after a manner," Prisius said.

Sperantus said to Halfpenny, "And you oatmeal groat, were you acquainted with this plot?"

Halfpenny is small, and an oatmeal groat — a single grain of oatmeal — is small.

"An accessary, as it were," Halfpenny said.

Sperantus said:

"Thou shall be punished as a principal."

Looking up, he said:

"Here come Memphio and Stellio. They likely were privy, and all their heads were laid together to grieve our hearts."

Memphio and his serving-boy, Dromio, entered the scene. So did Stellio and his serving-boy, Risio.

Memphio said, "Come, Stellio, the assurance — the financial settlement — may be made tomorrow, and our children assured — betrothed — today."

The fathers had arranged for their children — Accius and Silena — to become engaged.

"Let the conveyance run as we agreed," Stellio said.

Prisius said, "You convey cleanly indeed, if cheating is clean — plain — dealing, for in the apparel of your children you have conveyed a marriage match between our children, which grieves us not a little."

"Convey" can mean 1) transfer property, or 2) cheat.

Memphio said, "In the apparel of your children, you have revealed the folly of our children, which shames us overmuch."

"But it does not matter," Stellio said about Accius and Silena. "Although they are fools, they are not beggars."

"And although our children are disobedient, they are not fools," Sperantus said about Candius and Livia.

"So now they tune their pipes," Dromio whispered to Risio.

They were warming up their voices for what could be a major shouting match.

"You shall hear 'sweet' music between a hoarse raven and a screech owl," Risio said.

Memphio said, "Neighbors, let us not vary and quarrel. Our serving-boys have played their cheating parts. I suspected no less at the tavern, where our four knaves met together."

"If it were knavery for four to meet in a tavern, your worships know well there were four others in a tavern," Risio said.

The others were the four fathers.

"This villain calls us knaves by craft," Stellio said.

Lucio said, "Truly I dare to swear that he used no craft but speaks and means plainly."

Sperantus said:

"This is worse.

"Come, Halfpenny, tell the truth and escape the rod — escape being beaten."

Halfpenny said, "It is as good to confess here while trussed — that is, with my breeches being held up — as at home with my hose about my heels."

His pants would be down as he was whipped at home.

Dromio said to Sperantus:

"Nay, I'll tell thee."

He then said to Halfpenny:

"For it will never become thee to utter it."

"Well, out with it!" Memphio said.

Dromio said:

"Memphio had a fool as his son, which Stellio did not know.

"Stellio had a fool as his daughter, which was unknown to Memphio.

"To cheat each other, they dealt with their serving-boys for a marriage match. They wanted their children — Accius and Silena — to marry.

"We met with Lucio and Halfpenny, who told the love between their masters' children. The young people were deeply in love, and the fathers were unwilling to consent."

The young people deeply in love were Candius and Livia.

Risio said:

"I'll take the tale by the end — the tail.

"Then we four met, which argued we were no mountains."

A proverb stated, "Friends may meet, but mountains never greet."

Risio continued:

"And in a tavern we met, which argued we were mortal."

Many mortals enjoy drinking.

Risio continued:

"And everyone in his wine told his day's work, which was a sign we did not forget our business.

"Seeing all our masters busy with plots, we determined a little to trouble the water before they drank, so that in the attire of your children our masters' 'wise' children' — Accius and Silena — revealed their good natures, and in the garments of our masters' children your children — Candius and Livia — made a marriage.

"This all stood upon — depended upon — us poor children and your young children to show that old folks may be overtaken — outsmarted — by children."

"Here's a 'child-ren' indeed!" Prisius said. "I'll never forget it."

A "ren" is a "run." The children — especially the serving-boys — had metaphorically run circles around the old fathers.

Memphio said:

"I will."

Memphio could forget his child's disobedience by forgiving and forgetting.

Memphio called:

"Accius, come forth."

Stellio said:

"I forgive all."

Stellio called:

"Silena, come forth."

Sperantus said to Prisius, "Neighbor, these things cannot be recalled; therefore, we might as well consent to our children's marriage, seeing in all our purposes we also missed the mark, for those two will match their children."

He wanted Prisius and him to forgive their children — Candius and Livia — for marrying without their fathers' permission.

Prisius said:

"Well, about that more soon."

He lowered his voice and said to Sperantus:

"We will not forgive them suddenly lest our ungracious youths think we dare do no other thing, but in truth their loves stir up natural feelings of fatherly love in me."

Accius and Silena entered the scene, each coming from his or her father's house.

Memphio said, "Come, Accius, thou must be married to Silena. How are thou minded about it?"

"What!" Accius said. "Married forever and ever?"

"Accius, what else?" Memphio asked.

"I shall never be able to endure it!" Accius said. "It will be so tedious!"

Stellio said, "Silena, thou must be betrothed to Accius, and thou must love him for thy husband."

"I would as willingly have a husband made out of rags," Silena said. "I prefer a rag doll to Accius."

"Why, Silena?" Stellio asked.

"Why, look how he looks," Silena said.

Accius had a reputation for being good-looking, but chances are, he was looking at her with distaste.

"If you will not marry me, another will," Accius said.

"I thank you for my old cap," Silena said.

In other words: Thanks for nothing.

"And if you are so lusty, lend me two shillings," Accius said.

"Lusty" can mean "joyful." It can also mean "arrogant."

"We are happy and fortunate," Prisius whispered to Sperantus. "We missed the foolish marriage match."

Memphio said to Accius, "Come, you shall immediately be contracted."

Memphio wanted the marriage contract — the betrothal — to take place.

Dromio said, "Contract their wits no more; they are shrunk close — that is, concealed — already."

Accius said, "Well, father, here's my hand. Strike the bargain."

"Must he lie with me?" Silena asked.

"No, Silena, he must lie by thee," Stellio said.

Both "lie with" and "lie by" can mean to 1) "lie beside," and 2) "have sex with."

Silena may have meant meaning #1 and Stellio may have meant meaning #2.

Accius said, "I shall give her the humble bee's kiss."

He would have sex with her. A "sting" can be a metaphor for a penis.

Vicinia entered the scene. With her were Maestius and Serena.

Vicinia said, "I forbid the banns."

She was declaring that the marriage of Accius and Silena must not take place.

"What!" Risio said. "Do thou think that they are rats, and do thou fear they shall be poisoned?"

"Bane" is poison.

"You do, Vicinia?" Memphio said. "Why?"

Vicinia said, "Pay attention. About eighteen years ago, I nursed thee a son, Memphio, and I nursed thee a daughter, Stellio."

"True," Stellio said.

"True," Memphio said.

Vicinia said:

"I had at that time two children of my own, and being poor, I thought it better to exchange them than kill them."

She is unlikely to have thought about murdering her children, but rather to have thought that they would die because of the effects of poverty. After all, she did not kill the children whom she exchanged with her own children.

Vicinia continued:

"I imagined if by a plot I could thrust my children into your houses, they would be well brought up in their youth, and wisely provided for in their age.

"Nature wrought with me and I wanted the best for my children, and when they were weaned, I sent to your homes my children instead of your children. And hitherto you have kept them as tenderly as if they had been yours.

"Growing in years, I found the children — your children — I kept at home to love each other dearly, at first like brother and sister, which I rejoiced at, but at length they became too forward in affection, which although inwardly I could not mislike, yet openly I seemed to disallow and disapprove."

Maestius and Serena were beginning to love each other more like boyfriend and girlfriend than like brother and sister.

Vicinia continued:

"They increased in their loving humors and fancies, and I did not cease to chastise them for their loose demeanors: their too-much love for each other. At last, it came to my ears that my son who was out with Memphio was a fool, and that my daughter who was out with Stellio was also unwise, and yet although they were brother and sister, there was a match being hammered — being devised — between them."

Vicinia's children were actually the simpletons Accius and Silena.

Memphio's son was actually Maestius.

Stellio's daughter was actually Serena.

"What monstrous tale is this?" Memphio asked.

"And I am sure that tale is incredible — it is unable to be believed," Stellio said.

"Let her end her discourse," Sperantus said. "Let her say what she has come here to say."

"I'll never believe it," Accius said.

"Hold thy peace," Memphio said. "Be quiet."

Vicinia said:

"My very bowels earned — that is, grieved — within me, that I should be author of such vile incest, a hindrance to lawful love."

If Accius and Silena were to marry, they would be committing incest because they were biologically brother and sister.

Vicinia continued:

"I went to the good old woman Mother Bombie to know the event and outcome of this practice, who told me this day I might prevent the danger, and upon submission escape the punishment. And so hither I have come to claim my children, although they are both fools, and to deliver to you two — Memphio and Stellio — your children, who are both loving.

"Is this possible?" Memphio said. "How shall we believe it?"

"It cannot sink into my head," Stellio said.

Vicinia said:

"This test cannot fail. Memphio, your son had a mole under his ear. I made a mole under my child's ear by art.

"You shall see it taken away with the juice of mandrake.

"Behold."

She used mandrake juice to rub away the mole behind Accius' ear.

Vicinia then said:

"Now for your biological son's mole: No herb can undo that which nature has done."

She tried but failed to rub away the mole behind Maestius' ear.

Maestius was the son of Memphio.

Vicinia then said:

"Your daughter, Stellio, has on her wrist a mole, which I counterfeited on my daughter's arm, and that you shall see taken away like the other."

She used mandrake juice to rub away the mole that was on Silena's wrist.

Serena was the daughter of Stellio.

Vicinia then said:

"Thus you see I do not dissemble, hoping you will pardon me, as I have pitied them."

She had pitied Maestius and Serena, and her pity (in addition to her wish to keep her biological children from committing incest) had helped her decide to reveal their true parentage.

Memphio, the father of Maestius, said, "This is my son, O fortunate Memphio!"

Stellio, the father of Serena, said, "This is my daughter, more than thrice happy Stellio!"

Maestius said, "How happy is Maestius, thou blessed Serena, who being neither children to poor parents, nor brother and sister by nature, may enjoy their love by consent of parents and nature."

Maestius and Serena could marry and enjoy their love: have sex together.

Accius said, "Wait! I'll not swap — exchange — my father for all this!"

Silena said:

"What! Do you think I'll be cheated of my father? I think I should not!

"Mother Bombie told me my father knew me not, my mother bore me not. She said that I was falsely bred [brought up], truly begot. A plague on Mother Bombie!"

Silena's biological father did not know her. Stellio's wife did not give birth to Silena.

Dromio said, "Mother Bombie told us we would be found cheaters, and in the end we would be cheated by cheaters. Well may thou fare, Mother Bombie."

The four serving-boys had been deceivers and they had been deceived by deceivers.

Vicinia had been the main deceiver. Other deceivers had been deceivers because they had not known their true familial relationships.

Risio said to Dromio, "I heard Mother Bombie say that thou shall die a beggar. Beware of Mother Bombie."

Yes, beware of Mother Bombie. What Mother Bombie predicts comes true.

"Why, have you all been with Mother Bombie?" Prisius asked.

"Yes, all, and as far as I can see Mother Bombie has foretold all," Lucio said.

Memphio, the father of Maestius, said, "Indeed, she is cunning, knowledgeable, and wise, never doing harm, but always practicing good. Seeing these things fall out thus, are you content, Stellio, that the marriage match should go forward?"

This marriage match was between their children: Maestius and Serena.

Stellio, the father of Serena, said, "Aye, I am content, with double joy, having found for a fool a wise maiden, and finding between them both the utmost love."

Prisius, the father of Livia, said:

"Then to end all jars, aka quarrels, our children's marriage matches shall stand with our good liking.

"Livia, enjoy Candius."

Sperantus, the father of Candius, said, "Candius, enjoy Livia."

Candius asked, "How shall we recompense fortune, which to our loves has added our parents' good wills?"

Maestius asked, "How shall we requite fortune, which to our loves has added lawfulness, and which to our poor estate has added a competent living?"

The biological parents of Maestius and Serena were financially well off. Maestius and Serena had gone from impoverished to comfortable.

Memphio said, "Vicinia, thy crime is pardoned, although the law would see it punished. We are content to keep Silena in the house with the new married couple."

Stellio said, "And I do maintain Accius in our house."

Accius and Selena would exchange "fathers." Memphio had been Accius' "father," and Stellio had been Selena's "father."

This is likely to be good for all of them. Accius had been spoiled in his home through being over-indulged. Selena was not a natural fool, but she had overweening pride.

In his new home, Accius would not be spoiled, and in her new home, Silena would be less proud.

Earlier, Mother Bombie had predicted about Maestius and Serena, "And both of you together must relieve a fool."

With different "parents," both Accius and Selena may cease to be fools.

But the fool who is relieved may be Vicenia, who had acted badly when she exchanged babies.

Vicinia said, "Come, my children, although fortune has not provided you with lands, yet you see you are not destitute of friends. I shall be eased of a charge both in purse and conscience. In conscience, I have revealed my lewd practice — my vile deception. In purse, I will have you kept of alms."

Vicinia's biological children — Accius and Silena — would be provided for by the charity of Memphio and Stellio.

Accius said to Silena, "Come, if you are my sister, it's the better for you."

"Come, brother, I think it's better than it was," Silena said. "I should have been but a bald — a bad — bride. I'll eat as much pie as if I had been married."

"Let's also forgive the knavery of our serving-boys since all turns to our good fortune," Memphio said.

"Agreed, all are pleased," Stellio said. "Now the serving-boys are unpunished."

The hackneyman, sergeant, and scrivener entered the scene.

"Nay, wait, don't forget about us, and do seek redress for our wrongs, or we'll complain to the mayor," the hackneyman said.

"What's the matter?" Prisius asked.

The hackneyman said:

"I arrested Memphio's serving-boy, Dromio, over a horse.

"After much mocking, at the request of his fellow wags I was happy to take a bond jointly of them all. They had me go into a tavern. There they made me, the scrivener, and the sergeant drunk. They pawned the sergeant's mace for the wine, and they sealed for me an obligation that is nothing to the purpose: It does not do what it is supposed to do.

"I ask you to read it."

Memphio said, "What imps these serving-boys are!"

He read the bond and then said:

"Why, by this bond you can demand nothing.

"Things done in drink may be repented in soberness, but not remedied."

Dromio said, "Sir, I have his acquittance of my debt, so let him sue his bond."

The hackneyman said, "I'll cry quittance — get even — with thee."

The sergeant said, "And so will I, or it shall cost me the laying on freely of my mace."

If he did not get even with Dromio, he would not be able to use his mace to beat Dromio because his mace had been pawned.

But if he did get even with Dromio, he would get his mace back, and he would beat Dromio with it.

The scrivener said, "And I'll give thee such a dash with a pen as shall cost thee many a pound, with such a *Noverint* as Cheapside can show none such!"

Noverint — "Let all men know" — is the formal beginning of a legal writ.

The scrivener would draw up legal documents that would cause Dromio much trouble.

"Do your worst!" Halfpenny said. "Our knaveries will revenge it upon your children's children."

Deuteronomy 5:9 states (King James Version):

9 *Thou shalt not bow down thyself unto them, nor serve them: for I the Lord thy God am a jealous God, visiting the iniquity of the fathers upon the children unto the third and fourth generation of them that hate me,*

"Thou boy!" Memphio said.

He then said to the hackneyman:

"We will pay for the hire of the horse. Don't be angry. The boys have been in a merry cozening — tricking — vein, for they have served their masters in the same way, but all must be forgotten.

"Now all are content except the poor fiddlers; they shall be sent for to perform at the marriage and they will have double fees."

"You need no more send for a fiddler to a feast than send for a beggar to a fair," Dromio said.

In other words: The fiddlers will show up, whether sent for or not.

"This day we will feast at my house," Stellio said.

"Tomorrow we will feast at my house," Memphio said.

"The next day we will feast at my house," Prisius said.

Sperantus said, "Then we will feast at my house the last day, and so on even terms — with all the fathers contributing — we will spend this week in good cheer."

Dromio said, "Then we would best be going while everyone is pleased, and yet these couples are not fully pleased until the priest will have done his worst."

The priest needed to perform the marriages, which were required after the betrothals, and then the couples could be fully satisfied in bed.

Risio said, "Come, Sergeant, we'll toss wine into our mouths all this week, and we will make thy mace arrest a boiled capon."

The sergeant said, "Say no more words about that at the wedding. If the mayor should know about it, I would be in danger of losing my job."

His mace had been pawned for alcohol.

Risio said, "Then be careful how you exert your authority over such people as we serving-boys are. Be careful how you give us a taste of your legal authority."

"If you mace us, we'll pepper you," Halfpenny said.

Mace and pepper are spices.

"Come, sister, the best thing is that we shall have good cheer these four days," Accius said to Silena.

"And be fools forever," Lucio said.

Silena said, "That's none of our upseekings!'

It is wise not to seek to be a fool.

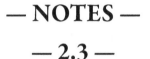

— NOTES —
— 2.3 —

Silena.

My father boards me already; therefore I care not if your name were Geoffrey.

(2.3.35-36)

Source of Above: Lyly, John. *Mother Bombie*. Ed. Leah Scragg. The Revels Plays. Manchester and New York: Manchester University Press, 2010. P. 101.

The phrase "Farewell gentle Geoffrey" appears in the play *Mankind*, where it is said by Nought, one of three unthrifty guests.

> *Nought.*
> *Go we hence, a devil way!*
> *Here is the door; here is the way!*
> *Farewell, gentle Geoffrey!*
> *I pray God give you good night!*
> [Exeunt three unthrifty guests: Nought, Now-a-Days, and New Guise.]
> *Mercy.*
> *Thanked be God! we have a fair deliverance*
> *Of these three unthrifty guests:*

Source of Above:

Mankind. Collected in *Early English Dramatists — Recently Recovered "Lost" Tudor Plays with some others, by Various*.
https://www.gutenberg.org/files/45805/45805-8.txt
A modern-spelling edition (with notes) appears here:
https://bidoonism.files.wordpress.com/2019/12/jhk___mankind_archive.pdf

— 2.3 —

Silena.

Aha, are you there with your bears?

(2.3.52)

Source of Above: Lyly, John. *Mother Bombie.* Ed. Leah Scragg. The Revels Plays. Manchester and New York: Manchester University Press, 2010. P. 101.

The paragraph below appears in the *Oxford English Dictionary* entry about the noun "bear":

> *[Explained in Joe Miller's Jests (1739) 28 as originally the exclamation of a man who, not liking a sermon he had heard on Elisha and the bears (2 Kings 2:23–4), went next Sunday to another church, only to find the same preacher and the same discourse.]*

The *Oxford English Dictionary* states that the joke is explained in *Joe Miller's Jests* (1739).

> *"123. A Gentleman hearing a Parson preach upon the Story of the Children being devoured by the two* She Bears, *who reviled the old Man, and not much liking his Sermon; some Time after seeing the same Parson come into the Pulpit to preach at another Church: O ho! said he,* What are you here with your Bears again."

Source: *Joe Miller's Jests, or The Wits Vade-Mecum.* Gutenberg edition.

https://www.gutenberg.org/ebooks/40127

The characters of Silena and Accius are interesting. They are simpletons, but they are probably not born fools. They seem to have been raised badly.

Silena's "bears" comment seems to make sense in the context of *Joe Miller's Jests*, but that book was published in 1739, and *Mother Bombie* was published in 1594. Was the joke current in 1594?

Memphio.

Ah! thy son will be begged for a concealed fool.

(4.2.121-122)

Source of Above: Lyly, John. *Mother Bombie*. Ed. Leah Scragg. The Revels Plays. Manchester and New York: Manchester University Press, 2010. P. 152.

There is a play on "concealed land":

King Henry VIII had dissolved the monasteries and taken their land, but some land that should have gone to the crown was concealed — the land that was taken from the monasteries and should have gone to the crown was instead held by private owners. Queen Elizabeth I gave commissions to people to find and report concealed land; these people received part or sometimes even all of the land. Some greedy people tried to claim that land legally owned by others was actually concealed land. These greedy people begged the land — they claimed they were entitled to part or all of the land as a reward.

APPENDIX A: FAIR USE

§ 107. Limitations on exclusive rights: Fair use

Release date: 2004-04-30

Notwithstanding the provisions of sections 106 and 106A, the fair use of a copyrighted work, including such use by reproduction in copies or phonorecords or by any other means specified by that section, for purposes such as criticism, comment, news reporting, teaching (including multiple copies for classroom use), scholarship, or research, is not an infringement of copyright. In determining whether the use made of a work in any particular case is a fair use the factors to be considered shall include —

(1) the purpose and character of the use, including whether such use is of a commercial nature or is for nonprofit educational purposes;

(2) the nature of the copyrighted work;

(3) the amount and substantiality of the portion used in relation to the copyrighted work as a whole; and

(4) the effect of the use upon the potential market for or value of the copyrighted work.

The fact that a work is unpublished shall not itself bar a finding of fair use if such finding is made upon consideration of all the above factors.

Source of Fair Use information:

http://www.law.cornell.edu/uscode/17/107.html

APPENDIX B: ABOUT THE AUTHOR

It was a dark and stormy night. Suddenly a cry rang out, and on a hot summer night in 1954, Josephine, wife of Carl Bruce, gave birth to a boy — me. Unfortunately, this young married couple allowed Reuben Saturday, Josephine's brother, to name their first-born. Reuben, aka "The Joker," decided that Bruce was a nice name, so he decided to name me Bruce Bruce. I have gone by my middle name — David — ever since.

Being named Bruce David Bruce hasn't been all bad. Bank tellers remember me very quickly, so I don't often have to show an ID. It can be fun in charades, also. When I was a counselor as a teenager at Camp Echoing Hills in Warsaw, Ohio, a fellow counselor gave the signs for "sounds like" and "two words," then she pointed to a bruise on her leg twice. Bruise Bruise? Oh yeah, Bruce Bruce is the answer!

Uncle Reuben, by the way, gave me a haircut when I was in kindergarten. He cut my hair short and shaved a small bald spot on the back of my head. My mother wouldn't let me go to school until the bald spot grew out again.

Of all my brothers and sisters (six in all), I am the only transplant to Athens, Ohio. I was born in Newark, Ohio, and have lived all around Southeastern Ohio. However, I moved to Athens to go to Ohio University and have never left.

At Ohio U, I never could make up my mind whether to major in English or Philosophy, so I got a bachelor's degree with a double major in both areas, then I added a Master of Arts degree in English and a Master of Arts degree in Philosophy. Yes, I have my MAMA degree.

Currently, and for a long time to come (I eat fruits and veggies), I am spending my retirement writing books such as *Nadia Comaneci: Perfect 10*, *The Funniest People in Comedy*, *Homer's* Iliad: *A Retelling in Prose*, and *William Shakespeare's* Hamlet: *A Retelling in Prose*.

If all goes well, I will publish one or two books a year for the rest of my life. (On the other hand, a good way to make God laugh is to tell Her your plans.)

By the way, my sister Brenda Kennedy writes romances such as *A New Beginning* and *Shattered Dreams*.

APPENDIX C: SOME BOOKS BY DAVID BRUCE

Retellings of a Classic Work of Literature

Ben Jonson's The Alchemist: *A Retelling*

Ben Jonson's The Arraignment, or Poetaster: *A Retelling*

Ben Jonson's Bartholomew Fair: *A Retelling*

Ben Jonson's The Case is Altered: *A Retelling*

Ben Jonson's Catiline's Conspiracy: *A Retelling*

Ben Jonson's The Devil is an Ass: *A Retelling*

Ben Jonson's Epicene: *A Retelling*

Ben Jonson's Every Man in His Humor: *A Retelling*

Ben Jonson's Every Man Out of His Humor: *A Retelling*

Ben Jonson's The Fountain of Self-Love, or Cynthia's Revels: *A Retelling*

Ben Jonson's The Magnetic Lady, or Humors Reconciled: *A Retelling*

Ben Jonson's The New Inn, or The Light Heart: *A Retelling*

Ben Jonson's Sejanus' Fall: *A Retelling*

Ben Jonson's The Staple of News: *A Retelling*

Ben Jonson's A Tale of a Tub: *A Retelling*

Ben Jonson's Volpone, or the Fox: *A Retelling*

Christopher Marlowe's Complete Plays: Retellings

Christopher Marlowe's Dido, Queen of Carthage: *A Retelling*

The Merry Devil of Edmonton: *A Retelling*

Robert Greene's Friar Bacon and Friar Bungay: *A Retelling*

The Taming of a Shrew: *A Retelling*

Tarlton's Jests: A Retelling

The Trojan War and Its Aftermath: Four Ancient Epic Poems

Virgil's Aeneid: *A Retelling in Prose*

William Shakespeare's 5 Late Romances: Retellings in Prose

William Shakespeare's 10 Histories: Retellings in Prose

William Shakespeare's 11 Tragedies: Retellings in Prose

William Shakespeare's 12 Comedies: Retellings in Prose

William Shakespeare's 38 Plays: Retellings in Prose

William Shakespeare's 1 Henry IV, aka Henry IV, Part 1: *A Retelling in Prose*

William Shakespeare's 2 Henry IV, aka Henry IV, Part 2: *A Retelling in Prose*

William Shakespeare's 1 Henry VI, aka Henry VI, Part 1: *A Retelling in Prose*

William Shakespeare's 2 Henry VI, aka Henry VI, Part 2: *A Retelling in Prose*

William Shakespeare's 3 Henry VI, aka Henry VI, Part 3: *A Retelling in Prose*

William Shakespeare's All's Well that Ends Well: *A Retelling in Prose*

William Shakespeare's Antony and Cleopatra: *A Retelling in Prose*

William Shakespeare's As You Like It: *A Retelling in Prose*

William Shakespeare's The Comedy of Errors: *A Retelling in Prose*

William Shakespeare's Coriolanus: *A Retelling in Prose*

William Shakespeare's Cymbeline: *A Retelling in Prose*

William Shakespeare's Hamlet: *A Retelling in Prose*

William Shakespeare's Henry V: *A Retelling in Prose*

William Shakespeare's Henry VIII: *A Retelling in Prose*

William Shakespeare's Julius Caesar: *A Retelling in Prose*

William Shakespeare's King John: *A Retelling in Prose*

William Shakespeare's King Lear: *A Retelling in Prose*

William Shakespeare's Love's Labor's Lost: *A Retelling in Prose*

William Shakespeare's Macbeth: *A Retelling in Prose*

William Shakespeare's Measure for Measure: *A Retelling in Prose*

William Shakespeare's The Merchant of Venice: *A Retelling in Prose*

William Shakespeare's The Merry Wives of Windsor: *A Retelling in Prose*

William Shakespeare's A Midsummer Night's Dream: *A Retelling in Prose*

William Shakespeare's Much Ado About Nothing: *A Retelling in Prose*

William Shakespeare's Othello: *A Retelling in Prose*

William Shakespeare's Pericles, Prince of Tyre: *A Retelling in Prose*

William Shakespeare's Richard II: *A Retelling in Prose*

William Shakespeare's Richard III: *A Retelling in Prose*

William Shakespeare's Romeo and Juliet: *A Retelling in Prose*

William Shakespeare's The Taming of the Shrew: *A Retelling in Prose*

William Shakespeare's The Tempest: A Retelling in Prose

William Shakespeare's Timon of Athens: A Retelling in Prose

William Shakespeare's Titus Andronicus: A Retelling in Prose

William Shakespeare's Troilus and Cressida: A Retelling in Prose

William Shakespeare's Twelfth Night: A Retelling in Prose

William Shakespeare's The Two Gentlemen of Verona: A Retelling in Prose

William Shakespeare's The Two Noble Kinsmen: A Retelling in Prose

William Shakespeare's The Winter's Tale: A Retelling in Prose

Other Fiction

Candide's Two Girlfriends (Adult)

Honey Badger Goes to Hell — and Heaven

I Want to Die — Or Fight Back

The Erotic Adventures of Candide (Adult)

Children's Biography

Nadia Comaneci: Perfect Ten

Personal Finance

How to Manage Your Money: A Guide for the Non-Rich

Anecdote Collections

250 Anecdotes About Opera

250 Anecdotes About Religion

250 Anecdotes About Religion: Volume 2

250 Music Anecdotes

Be a Work of Art: 250 Anecdotes and Stories

The Coolest People in Art: 250 Anecdotes

The Coolest People in the Arts: 250 Anecdotes

The Coolest People in Books: 250 Anecdotes

The Coolest People in Comedy: 250 Anecdotes

Create, Then Take a Break: 250 Anecdotes

Don't Fear the Reaper: 250 Anecdotes

The Funniest People in Art: 250 Anecdotes

The Funniest People in Books: 250 Anecdotes

The Funniest People in Books, Volume 2: 250 Anecdotes

The Funniest People in Books, Volume 3: 250 Anecdotes

The Funniest People in Comedy: 250 Anecdotes

The Funniest People in Dance: 250 Anecdotes

The Funniest People in Families: 250 Anecdotes

The Funniest People in Families, Volume 2: 250 Anecdotes

The Funniest People in Families, Volume 3: 250 Anecdotes

The Funniest People in Families, Volume 4: 250 Anecdotes

The Funniest People in Families, Volume 5: 250 Anecdotes

The Funniest People in Families, Volume 6: 250 Anecdotes

The Funniest People in Movies: 250 Anecdotes

The Funniest People in Music: 250 Anecdotes

The Funniest People in Music, Volume 2: 250 Anecdotes

The Funniest People in Music, Volume 3: 250 Anecdotes

The Funniest People in Neighborhoods: 250 Anecdotes

The Funniest People in Relationships: 250 Anecdotes

The Funniest People in Sports: 250 Anecdotes

The Funniest People in Sports, Volume 2: 250 Anecdotes

The Funniest People in Television and Radio: 250 Anecdotes

The Funniest People in Theater: 250 Anecdotes

The Funniest People Who Live Life: 250 Anecdotes

The Funniest People Who Live Life, Volume 2: 250 Anecdotes

The Kindest People Who Do Good Deeds, Volume 1: 250 Anecdotes

The Kindest People Who Do Good Deeds, Volume 2: 250 Anecdotes

Maximum Cool: 250 Anecdotes

The Most Interesting People in Movies: 250 Anecdotes

The Most Interesting People in Politics and History: 250 Anecdotes

The Most Interesting People in Politics and History, Volume 2: 250 Anecdotes

The Most Interesting People in Politics and History, Volume 3: 250 Anecdotes

The Most Interesting People in Religion: 250 Anecdotes

The Most Interesting People in Sports: 250 Anecdotes

The Most Interesting People Who Live Life: 250 Anecdotes

The Most Interesting People Who Live Life, Volume 2: 250 Anecdotes

Reality is Fabulous: 250 Anecdotes and Stories

Resist Psychic Death: 250 Anecdotes

Seize the Day: 250 Anecdotes and Stories

Discussion Guide Series

Dante's Inferno: *A Discussion Guide*

Dante's Paradise: *A Discussion Guide*

Dante's Purgatory: *A Discussion Guide*

Forrest Carter's The Education of Little Tree: *A Discussion Guide*

Homer's Iliad: *A Discussion Guide*

Homer's Odyssey: *A Discussion Guide*

Jane Austen's Pride and Prejudice: *A Discussion Guide*

Jerry Spinelli's Maniac Magee: *A Discussion Guide*

Jerry Spinelli's Stargirl: *A Discussion Guide*

Jonathan Swift's "A Modest Proposal": A Discussion Guide

Lloyd Alexander's The Black Cauldron: *A Discussion Guide*

Lloyd Alexander's The Book of Three: *A Discussion Guide*

Lloyd Alexander's The Castle of Llyr: *A Discussion Guide*

Mark Twain's Adventures of Huckleberry Finn: *A Discussion Guide*

Mark Twain's The Adventures of Tom Sawyer: *A Discussion Guide*

Mark Twain's A Connecticut Yankee in King Arthur's Court: *A Discussion Guide*

Mark Twain's The Prince and the Pauper: *A Discussion Guide*

Nancy Garden's Annie on My Mind: *A Discussion Guide*

Nicholas Sparks' A Walk to Remember: *A Discussion Guide*

Virgil's Aeneid: *A Discussion Guide*